DINNY
AND THE
WITCHES

THE
MIRACLE
WORKER

DINNY AND THE WITCHES

TWO PLAYS BY

WILLIAM GIBSON

NEW YORK ATHENEUM PUBLISHERS

THE MIRACLE WORKER

for the wife and the kids and the next breath

with love

CONTENTS

Prefatory: A Hit and a Flop

PAGE 3

Dinny and the Witches

PAGE 23

The Miracle Worker

PAGE 157

DINNY
AND THE
WITCHES

THE
MIRACLE
WORKER

PREFATORY:

A HIT AND A FLOP

AMONG THE MANY PROVISIONS I have made for my declining years, so prematurely upon me since my first encounter with the professional theatre, I find none for defending in public my wish to have two more plays produced. Normally the wish would hardly need justification. But last year I published a theatre log which so many readers took as an exit speech that they were convinced I must be embarrassed to meet myself onstage again; they were, for me. Readers of that log of course know something of the history of *The Miracle Worker*, and how it was promised to a director, producer, and actress before I knew what I was saying, a mitigation which does not extend to *Dinny and the Witches*. Both plays, however, in conception and initial writing, antedate the log, and rewriting and producing them have been for me a matter chiefly of cleaning up behind me. Whether the log was meant as an exit speech is something I am still waiting to hear from higher—or perhaps I mean lower: in any case intravisceral—authorities.

Meanwhile some gossip about the two plays in relation to the log may serve to engage the reader's interest and extricate the author's. Their character and fate could not have been more disparate. One was a recent piece, the other an early; one was a documentary, the other a fantasia; one was produced on Broadway, budgeted at $125,000, and the other off, at $15,000; one was an uneventful birth, the other convulsive with mishaps; one at this writing is running to standing room only, and the other is only running this preface a neck-and-neck race to a close. The most notable difference to me was in their origin. I was of course happy that one was a hit, and not happy that the other was not, but neither feeling ran too deep; the extremes of failure and success in the theatre are pathological, and perhaps equally destructive to its artists, each of whom must bring his own umbrella against the onslaught. Mine was the fact that the early play was born from the inside out, a matter of art, good or bad, and the later from the outside in, a matter of craft, good or bad, and under the knowledge of that difference I could weather the compliments with as little credence as the insults.

Dinny and the Witches was originally written in 1945 as a one-act play, and produced by a Topeka community theatre I was active in; its content more or less comprised that of the present first act, minus the songs. I had been in something of a despair for a time, and professionally in one of those paralyses every writer knows, when a locking of horns within him leaves him speechless, till presently the horns marry and have offspring, some bawling insight which reconciles opposites, and the writer scurries for a form to swaddle it in. Such as it was—I was very young in 1945, only two or three years old—my insight then was that discontentment is our nature. It tumbled out in some angry poems I wrote that fall—

> *Skin like a net on the mad eels of muscle that*
> *   kick*
> *In these runnels of limb, I am caught*

> *And snarled, wrist to knee,*
> *In its trammels: hanged in and gnarling it, gut*
> *   sick*
> *And cut by it, fouling it taut,*
> *   At wit's end I see*
> *This net is me, this net is me:*

—but then I wanted to say the same thing with joy. I had been contemplating *Dinny* as poetic drama, but I was delivered from that monstrosity by one ludicrous image, that of the baby carriage rolling in out of nowhere, and I rolled with it into all the improvisatory and colloquial absurdities of the one act. When it was staged, a friend asked his ten-year-old daughter what she thought Dinny was really looking for, and she said, "I think he was looking for that girl he left." The act said no, but the child was better informed, and around 1950 I was equal to her insight, if not to the baby carriage.

In that year I came around to another despair, and again *Dinny* sprang to my rescue. It sprang almost faster than I could put it down, three weeks of quasi-automatic writing in a fever of last-ditch optimism, two new acts and the first revised, jumping with songs, dances, and funny sayings, gallows gaiety and a gallows affirmation of the world as it is, but with the tongue of that collaborating child in its cheek, a naïve, ridiculous, affectionate roundelay to being alive. I regarded it as an eminently commercial piece of writing, and I was much astonished when no one produced it. It was my fifth full-length astonishment.

Three years later I had an unwitting glimpse of my seventh, when I put *The Miracle Worker* on paper as

the sparest of narratives. I had volunteered to write a
text to accompany a solo dancer, chose for a theme
Helen Keller, and in rereading her autobiography first
came upon Annie Sullivan's letters in its appendix. I
thought them among the most extraordinary letters I
had ever read, and I drew the dance text—as later I did
the play—almost exclusively from them.

I knew little enough then of their author. An editorial
note leading into the letters stated she had been "almost totally blind" from early in life, until in her teens
"her sight was partially restored"; later I learned it was
by painful and repeated surgery, under charitable aus-
pices. She was graduated in 1886 from the Perkins Institution for the Blind, in Boston, and that year was
recommended to an Alabama family as teacher to their
six-year-old daughter. The child is portrayed in the letters. Having lost in infancy sight, hearing, and the re-
sources of language, she had lived ever since like an
animal—worse, with a soul, shackled, wild with rages
and despair. Annie arrived in Tuscumbia on March 3,
1887, with the staggering task of putting this deaf,
mute, blind bundle of fierce flesh in touch with all human intelligence. She was twenty years old. One month
later, on April 5, she set into that small hungry hand
the understanding of words as symbolic thought and
"key to everything she wants to know."

The phrase is Annie's. Much about her is deducible
from the letters, which were written to a kind of foster
mother at Perkins, and begin three days after Annie
entered the Keller household; eight letters give the de-
tails of that first month, and thirty others take us to
May, 1888, when Annie and Helen left Tuscumbia for
Perkins and the world. She says of herself

When I sit down to write, my thoughts
freeze, and when I get them on paper they
look like wooden soldiers all in a row, and if
a live one happens along, I put him in a strait-
jacket

but the style belies it; we are at once in the presence of
a girl of wit, a talent for words, and a self-respect which
does not need fictions:

I appreciate the kind things Mr. Anagnos
has said . . . but . . . why . . . does he take
the trouble to ascribe motives to me that I
never dreamed of? You know, and he knows,
and I know, that my motive in coming here
was not in any sense philanthropic. . . . I
came here simply because circumstances made
it necessary for me to earn my living.

And audacity: in the teeth of such circumstances

I shall stand between her and the overindul-
gence of her parents. I have told Captain and
Mrs. Keller that they must not interfere with
me in any way.

And her own fierce flesh:

I had a battle royal with Helen this morning. . . . Helen's table manners are appalling.
She puts her hands in our plates and . . .
takes out whatever she wants. This morning I
would not let her put her hand in my plate.
She persisted, and a contest of wills followed.

Naturally the family was much disturbed, and
left the room. I locked the dining-room door,
and proceeded to eat my breakfast, though the
food almost choked me. Helen was lying on
the floor, kicking and screaming and trying to
pull my chair from under me. She kept this up
for half an hour, then she got up to see what I
was doing. I let her see that I was eating, but
did not let her put her hand in the plate. She
pinched me, and I slapped her every time she
did it. Then she went all around the table to
see who was there, and finding no one but me,
she seemed bewildered. . . . She . . . began
to eat her breakfast with her fingers. I gave her
a spoon, which she threw on the floor. I forced
her out of the chair and made her pick it up.
Finally I succeeded in getting her back in her
chair . . . and held the spoon in her hand,
compelling her to take up the food with it and
put it in her mouth. . . . Then we had another tussle over folding her napkin. When
she had finished she threw it on the floor and
ran toward the door. Finding it locked, she began to kick and scream all over again. It was
another hour before I succeeded in getting her
napkin folded. Then I let her out into the
warm sunshine and went up to my room and
threw myself on the bed exhausted. I had a
good cry and felt better.

And its ills:

My eyes are very much inflamed.

And simple genius:

> I am beginning to suspect all elaborate and
> special systems of education. They seem to me
> to be built up on the supposition that every
> child is a kind of idiot who must be taught to
> think. Whereas, if the child is left to himself,
> he will think more and better, if less showily.
> Let him go and come freely, let him touch real
> things and combine his impressions for him-
> self, instead of sitting indoors . . . while a
> sweet-voiced teacher suggests that he . . .
> plant straw trees in bead flower-pots. Such
> teaching fills the mind with artificial associa-
> tions that must be got rid of, before the child
> can develop independent ideas out of actual
> experiences.

That this principle and its practice, foredating by a
generation or more an entire school of progressive edu-
cators, should come from a girl of twenty is startling
enough; what is incredible is that six years earlier the
girl herself had been sightless, an inmate of the garbage
pile which was the state poorhouse, and totally illiter-
ate.

But that is another story, told for the first time in
Nella Braddy's *Anne Sullivan Macy*, a chest of jewels I
was not to open for three more years. In 1953, the
dance for which I prepared the text evaporated, and I
was left with twelve pages of narration on my hands.

I came back to *Dinny and the Witches* the following
spring, to see it through a local amateur production,

budgeted at $75. I rewrote the middle of it, took out a quantity of what my wife called my "personal debris," and eliminated the act-breaks, yoking it all together in one scene that ran two hours, with the concealed act-climaxes about as secret within as a camel's humps; in this form it was subsequently produced in a few summer and university theatres. Though the rewriting was now altogether external, I was no less fond of the piece, and it made some friends.

We had meanwhile acquired a baby carriage of our own, and in the summer of 1956 we had two things in sight, another occupant for it and no income; a sixth play I had just written called *Two for the Seesaw* was being rejected by the cleverest producers in the business. In desperation I mailed the twelve pages of dance text to a friend, the director Arthur Penn, asking was there not a television script and some money in them? Penn phoned me forty-eight hours later to say the television script was sold, for summer airing, and how soon could I put in ten days writing it? I said that since I had never written for television, and did not own a set, he had better come up to describe the medium to me. It took us a few hours to lay out the action together, and I spent the next month and a half clothing this prospectus in dialogue and my new son's retrospectus in diapers. I thus missed the summer deadline; but when I read the script to friends I saw I had at least not ruined one of the great stories of the world. It was Penn who against much official mucilage promoted *The Miracle Worker* to winter sponsorship, under which he directed it in February, 1957, to a furor of applause, and I have been referred to ever since as a graduate of the television industry. In terms of time invested, I believe this is grossly unfair to the diaper industry. My chief feeling about the script itself was rather apologetic: I thought it a skimpy piece of writing, in no way adequate to the woman I had now altogether lost my heart to in Nella Braddy's book.

After the telecast, while chewing my fingernails over what seemed the fading likelihood of a *Seesaw* production, I turned my thoughts to other income from this script. There was much buzzing about picture deals, but only one offer came out of it, a sizable sum, but hand in hand with a movie star I could not visualize as the woman I loved; after two or three weeks of oscillating between the actress and the money I said no, and felt lighthearted again. Late that summer I had lunch with an impressivario—I mean an actual producer, with shows, an office, a staff, and a phone number—whom I found charming and intelligent: he said he wished to option *The Miracle Worker* for immediate stage production, and how soon could I put in one week polishing it? I went home and put in three weeks rewriting the first act of it for the stage, concluded it was workable, and wrote so to the producer, who at once disappeared out of my life. This evaporation left me with one act of a stage play on my hands; I was making progress.

So was the casting of *Seesaw*, which with a beard a year and a half long at last went into production. During rehearsals another movie offer for *The Miracle Worker* came my way, this one giving me some control of casting, but now I could not think of that first act going to waste; I declined the movie, and exercised my right to cancel a second telecast, by way of keeping some audience at least theoretically available. It is noteworthy that every noble decision I made against sure money paid off a hundredfold, proving it hardly pays nowadays to be ignoble, even in the theatre, and I presently made another. After one week of anguish on the road with *Seesaw* I knew enough about its producer and actress regardless of our fate to offer *The Miracle Worker* to the two of them, with Penn's concurrence as director. After six weeks on the road, and our New York victory, I wished never to lay eyes on any of them again. I had made alas too much progress, I now had a first act, a director, a producer, an actress, and a successful theatre début on my hands; there was no turning back.

Accordingly I turned back, and spent six months writing a case history of *Two for the Seesaw*. I had several motives in undertaking that anatomy. In the opinion of some friends, the year or more I had worked on the play would have been invested more wisely in clearing our back hill of rocks and raising edible roots, and it was only its reception almost two years later that allowed me to discard this plan. I was still quaking, however; I quaked more vigorously over success than over failure, and the sole purgative I found was in reliving, on paper, the events of those two years. These shuddering ups and downs I tabulated and published under a title of debatable wit but metaphoric accuracy, *The Seesaw Log*.

It was never a question in my mind whether the log was in bad taste: I knew it was, and friends who read it in manuscript suggested that its entire contents be deleted prior to publication. They thought it too vindictive, too generous, too guilt-laden, too blameless, too self-pitying, and too harsh upon its author to warrant

any hope that anyone in the theatre would ever work
with me again. I have of course no enemies, but I do
have some curious friends, and it baffles me what they
see in each other. What they were supposed to see in
the log was the physiognomy of our theatre. I began it
as a biography of a playscript, from its conception on
through its metamorphoses by all hands present, author,
producer, director, actors, and out-of-town critics and
audiences; the book lacked only a variorum text of these
changes in toto, but I had the last-minute modesty to
spare its readers my junked dialogue. It grew inevitably
into a day-by-day chronicle of a show in rehearsal and
on the road, complete with financial and personal break-
downs, thus making a splendid theatre manual for anyone considering this field of endeavor as an alternative
to trapeze work without nets. It meandered into autobiography, with touching glimpses of my family life
and diet. It sank to profound, even bottomless, medita-
tions upon the consequences of the collaborative nature
of the theatre arts. It ended as mourning music.

What it mourned was the passing of a theatre which
had never existed. It had flourished only in my head, in
my ignorance of the economics of show business; with
my baptismal dip into this sulphuric front, my ideal
and personal reserve went up in smoke together. The
fact is, I entered the theatre thinking of it as a church,
and emerged thinking of it as a brothel. Now if either
of these views is justified, both are. The dilemma into
which I squeezed at the end of my tale seemed to be
whether to join the ministry or open a house of ill
repute; it was not inconceivable I might accomplish
both ends simultaneously with another play.

In truth, another play was possible only after the log

was written. Among its motives, perhaps its principal
one escaped notice, though it will be comprehended by
everyone who has survived the blight of success: to
separate myself ungraciously and violently from that of
Seesaw was a necessary condition for further work. I
expected and expect it to take forms not limited to
drama, but there I was, with a first act rotting on the
vine, with three friends waiting, a producer, director,
and actress, whose own logs of their troubles with me
were unwritten only because they had been too busy
earning my royalties to find the time, and with the
foreknowledge that the underlying story of *The Miracle
Worker* would be as irresistible at the box office as it
had been on television. Much more personally, I had
been burned too ingloriously during *Seesaw*, and I had
to hold my hand in that fire again; I was reared by
Indians in the Bronx.

I estimated six weeks would see me through the second and third acts, and they took me six months. True,
it was all craft and lethargized me, but that I needed
five times as long to rewrite as I had for the original
script was a technical matter as well. The camera is the
most facile medium in the world to write for; with the
free run of time and place it can untie one story knot at
a time and skip on, and has such transparency as a medium that it not only does not need, but is burdened by,
too many words; it offers as little resistance to the writer,
and as little home, as any lady of easy virtue. The stage
is as demanding as a wife. It can, indeed must, be lived
with, to come at its riches; its unit of time is not the
single moment, but the prolonged scene, in which so
many knots are concurrent that their ordering is as
rigorous as polyphony; and not owning a transparent

and mobile eye, it is less a medium than a vessel, empty
without the writer's substance. My impressivario who
had allotted me one week to translate from camera to
stage would, given my compliance, have blown his
brains out in the second week of rehearsals.

The spinal scenes of course stood, being factual; I
had invented almost nothing of Helen's, or of what
passes between her and Annie, though in every scene
I had brought together incidents separated in actual
time. What the stage needed was meatier people in a
wider reverberation of those incidents. I had two con-
ceptual poles for this: everyone in the family was to be
significantly affected by the work with the child, and
we were to see it liberate the teacher from her past as
much as the pupil from her present. For the first, I had
to invent connective tissue, in characterizations and
relationships, but without the license to make them
unconditionally mine; the material was awkwardly
placed in history, too far away for documentary truth
and too close for fictional. For the second, I introduced
moments when Annie was haunted by the voices of
memory, and quoted those which after sixty years she
could still summon up—and first did, toward the end of
her life, for Nella Braddy's ear. Though I wrote them
solely for the stage, we never arrived in production at a
satisfactory presentation of these voices; economy re-
quired that they be done on tape instead of live, and
half of the reviewers, for lack of other information,
deplored this transplant from the television script. My
own complaint was more pervasive: when a piece of
writing fails to flower in an individuality of verbal
idiom—or what a literary friend called "personal
aroma"—something is wrong at its roots. But I had

done my utmost, within the limits of the volition which
is craft, and in any case my aroma seemed less historic
than the events I was serving as secretary to.

Halfway through this chore, an old acquaintance
asked permission to produce and direct *Dinny and the
Witches* off-Broadway. After *Seesaw* I had instructed
my agent to hide my earlier plays; I was unwilling to
have *Dinny* seen without a rewrite and unwilling to
rewrite, but in the end I rewrote; I could not then any
more than now deny Dinny his chance in public, and
off-Broadway seemed the place for him. As soon as *The
Miracle Worker* was off my desk I restored *Dinny* to
three acts, and wrote some new material for the second.
I felt this play did not lack aroma, but the laws of its
structure and texture had been laid down in its first
emergence fourteen years before, and they lacked much
I had become cognizant of since; rewriting is no sub-
stitute for the original act, and there are values that are
achieved in first creation or never.

My past, thus backing up into the present, over-
flowed into the second half of 1959 with the presentation of two new plays, respectively three and nine years
less than new; neither had been written as any kind of
previsionary answer to the later log, nor did their show-
ing mean I had repented me of anything I wrote
therein, but I expected in these productions uptown
and down to learn something additional, and I did.

Uptown, I learned how the playwright can avoid the
agonies that lend Broadway its special lack of charm.
The production of *The Miracle Worker* was a painless
operation, the formula for which must represent a
breakthrough comparable to that of a cancer cure; I
make it available here to all. First, the play in manu-

script should be an assured hit; without this, nothing
can be done. With it, and a preceding hit, the producing team will be obliged to fight off money like hornets,
and can cast the play with an eye to more than bribing
backers and theatre owners. Secondly, the author should
enter rehearsals only in a state of financial independence, so that he may have a free mind for the work at
hand, which is to play tennis while the actors are com-
mitting their initial crimes. Thirdly, the police, that is,
the director and producer, should be intimates chosen
by the playwright for their perspicacity in recognizing
murder when they see it; strangers, however eminent,
will not do. Fourthly, the star should not only be able
to act—I know some of these conditions seem utopian
—but be, like the others, a rational human being.
Fifthly, the playwright should advise all concerned that
he will make visits to but not be in residence with the
show on the road prior to New York, and any rewriting
truly needed will be taken home to the comforts of his
customary workplace; in short, he will not live the hotel
life. This provision may be waived by authors who do
not visualize hell as a hotel room, but it will open them
to the twenty-four-hour fallout of anxiety which is the
only predictable manna of the profession. Sixthly, the
playwright should have just published a log of his preceding play; the threat of another day-by-day record in
progress will keep his co-workers polite in their approaches to him. Seventhly, the show should be greeted
by invariable ovations on the road, so that the reviewers
waiting in New York may order their minds in respect-
ful attitudes.

Having wisely arranged matters thus, we found *The
Miracle Worker* an era of peace and prosperity; the re-

viewers almost unanimously instructed their readers to
come, and everyone who could read came.

Downtown, I learned—among many other things—
what the audience is. The production of *Dinny and the
Witches* was a rich and varied inexperience, a detailing
of which would not augment my reputation for credibil-
ity, culminating in the news just prior to opening
that our theatre had no fire permit under which to
operate. For ten days we marched around in a circle,
while the folks at home wittily said, "Mr. Gibson is
going to throw another log on the Fire Department,"
and we then moved into another theatre; but those ten
days were a labor of love and education.

For several of them the cast, valiantly ignoring fire
inspectors, lawsuits, box-office seizures, countersuits, and
official threats to put our entire audience behind bars,
played "previews." Each of our first three audiences sat
like a houseful of wax manikins, and the occupational
shudders of being unwanted nuisances overtook us all.
In no other medium is there so little hiding place from
the audience, or is the artist's marriage to it so internally
joined in him; the instant his work is set naked before it
he becomes one with his audience, sees every moment
anew with its eyes, and is ready to break faith with
whatever fails to "work"—an everyhour word in show
business, meaning to visibly enrapture the spectator.
Now such disequilibrium in the artist's sights is precisely
what we mean by corruption, but it has its own integ-
rity, too. It is a psychic alteration of some complexity,
yet all of a piece, running back to the communicative
need which in every artist antecedes even the fantasy
which antecedes his art; his fantasies, unlike others',
imply a public. In fleshing his work forth, he keeps one

eye on the matter welling up in him, which is personal, and the other eye on its form, which is not, or he would communicate with no one; his awareness of form bespeaks his awareness of audience; still, if in this phase he favors either, it had better be—and usually is—his matter. But with its unveiling in the theatre its private character dies, even to him, and the need for communicatees reclaims its imperious seat in his mind; both his eyes unite with the spectator's, and the cycle is complete. This process is an absolute in the medium of our drama, and it begins and ends in the artist's compulsion to mastery, of himself and his public, not in the commercial rewards which are only a happy corollary. I was up to my eyeballs in this relationship to the spectator with our first houseful of manikins. I had taken refuge from it in *Seesaw* behind a most knowledgeable director and producer, who reacted instinctively wtih the audience and whom I could thus ungratefully bracket with it as enemy aliens; in *The Miracle Worker* the audience was ours from the first minute on; but in *Dinny* I could not blink the fact that the connection was mine to establish or nobody's. Accordingly we dug into work —restaged, cut, rewrote—and with our fourth performance the audience unfroze, joined us, wept a little, laughed a lot, and de-iced our hearts with curtain-call applause; the show was alive.

We worked thereafter in a warm give-and-take with each preview houseful, laboring by day on what it revealed to us by night, fed by its responding to the play much as I hoped it would. True, some disliked the script, or the production, or both, but the prevailing wind was favorable: we received enthusiastic fan mail, other off-Broadway managements told ours we had a

hit, and a reporter from one of the weeklies informed
his office he had seen a show that "would run for three
years." I also got an indignant letter requesting a refund
of the ticket price; I refunded it.

By these and more interior standards, *Dinny and the
Witches* was a success, but the reviewers were a flop.
Four out of seven experienced the play as a pretentious
bore. Perhaps it would have looked otherwise to them
in the cozy informality of our original theatre, where we
had designed for and mastered the space, playing in the
three-quarters round at the very ankles of the spectators;
when the authorities closed its doors and we moved to
the remote severity of a proscenium stage, with four
days to build new scenery and seven to reconceive the
show, we lost the play of farcicality with the audience;
we opened to another theatreful of manikins. But we
drew some affirmative responses also; one reviewer,
whom I cannot not quote, thought the play "from start
to finish a delightful, disarming, and delectable romp
. . . a continual fun-fest, replete with outrageous puns,
wild images, exceedingly clever dialogue, brilliant situa-
tions, and hundreds of novel, irreverent switches on the
sane and the conventional . . . the funniest, most
original play to come around in a long time." This re-
view seemed to me wise, temperate, objective, well-
reasoned, and from start to finish a continual fun-fest.
Alas, the more influential if less playful reviewers instructed their readers to stay away, and everyone who
could read stayed away. But I do not mean to twit the
reviewers; one must remember that they too are only
human, at their best.

In the week between theatres, we rehearsed *Dinny*
in a silence which was oddly sterile. It was my first ex-

perience with a show which, having been shaped in
some rapport with an audience, was then further
worked upon without one; I told some of the cast it
felt to me like an uprooted tree, all of whose leaves
were withering for lack of its mother soil. For better
or worse, the audience is that soil.

Clearly, with its part so organic to the theatrical act,
the playwright would do well to choose his audience as
carefully as his other collaborators, the director and actors. Can he? The Broadway audience is a given. It
has grown monolithic; a generation ago, when thirty
plays could be produced for what one musical comedy
costs now, they could survive on fractions of this audience, but *The Miracle Worker* must attract a thousand theatregoers a night or close; there is little choice
here. In domiciling *Dinny* off Broadway, I was aiming
at a different public from that needed uptown, possibly
with other values, certainly one-tenth its size. If such an
audience existed for or was deserved by the play, we
failed to reach it. Obviously I am not the person to
assay deserts here, and I humbly defer to the reviewers
who found the play wanting. Yet it is not irrelevant
that the manager of our off-Broadway theatre, speaking
of a Beckett play that had run there for six weeks of
successful previews, said their "only mistake was in
opening for the critics," with the implication that if it
had never opened it would still be running; and the
problem of how to reach another audience, through
daily reviewers whose taste on the whole so responsibly
mirrors the Broadway audience and its values, remains.
But it is only an incidental problem. The Broadway
audience is the nation's; it is our only audience which
exists in numbers sufficient to support a complete thea-

tre, from playwrights to ticket-takers; it is therefore the audience to which every germinating talent in the theatre is drawn. All other audiences—off-Broadway, at our universities, in little-theatre communities—are second-best and temporary substitutes. It is not dominant in the American grain to regard less money, less glory, and for that matter working conditions of less technical finish, as preferable to more, merely for the sake of internal scope. If *Dinny* had been a hit, it would have lost its entire personnel to better jobs uptown; the new playwrights who create any stir downtown promote themselves to Broadway at best, to television at worst, and come to terms with the needs of that enveloping audience; the movement is as irreversible as rivers flowing to the sea.

I do not know that this is only regrettable. It means losses, certainly, but the drama is a popular art or it is nothing; and the main stream of significant theatre writing in this country—as in all places and times—has been only for the public with money in its hand. Elite critics who with good reason lament the truncations of talent in the market-place theatre somehow miss the subjective crux, that its practitioners and audience cannot but be one, and no summons to reform over the audience's heads will alter anything. If all our teachers from kindergarten up were Annie Sullivans, we would be a different people, and my own theatre reform calls only for trebling the salary of every teacher in the union without a moment's delay. To put it most extremely, it is ultimately our audiences who write our plays, and a simple choice exists in the face of that immutable fact: take it or leave it.

                                                    —W. G.

DINNY
AND THE
WITCHES

A FROLIC ON GRAVE MATTERS

*"I mean, who wouldn't make a love song to
the world, at its worst, the day it died?"*
—BEN

THIS PLAY *happens in Central Park. The time is now, and again.*

AT THE SIDE OF THE STAGE *a flipper, moved in and out as needed in each act, suggests a grubby entrance to a night club called The Fission Hole. The body of the stage is the park itself, with a tipsy street lamp, a couple of trees, some rocks, a hillock, and a park bench. In the background loom the skyline buildings of the city.*

THE SET AND COSTUMES *should be improvisatory, and match the comic-strip horseplay of the action. The stage-wall bricks painted black, with a skyline sketched like a child's blackboard drawing in colored chalk, would be most apt; the stage pieces and props should come from a junk yard; costuming should be minimal, and avoid the fantastic like the plague. The physical materials of the show should be everyday, anti-poetic, and playful, and if they cost in all more than ninety-eight dollars, they are esthetically wrong. Dinny's horn can of course be another instrument, such as a clarinet; if its sound is to be dubbed from offstage, the instrument should be fashioned out of wire cloth and be manifestly unreal.*

ACT I

IT IS LATE AT NIGHT, AND THE PARK IS EMPTY. AN AN-
NOUNCER'S VOICE INTRODUCES THE PLAY, AS FOLLOWS:

"*Ladies and gentlemen. Inasmuch as the management
can assume no responsibility for recent progress in ap-
plied nuclear research, we think it best to open each
performance with our curtain calls, to be sure of getting
them in. There will be no general call at its conclusion,
if reached; run, do not walk, to the nearest exit. Here-
with the characters, in the order of their disappearance:*

"———————— *as* DAWN;

———————— *as* CHLOE;

———————— *as* BUBBLES (ALGONQUIN 4–6099);

———————— *as* BEN;

———————— *as* JAKE;

———————— *as* STONEHENGE;

———————— *as* TOM;

———————— *as* DICK;

———————— *as* HARRY;

———————— *as* DINNY;

———————— *as* AMY;

———————— *as* LUELLA;

———————— *as* ULGA;

———————— *as* ZENOBIA."

*Each character as named enters, bows, and continues
off, until* DINNY *appears. He does not bow, but pauses
to admire the night sky;* AMY *comes on behind him,
pauses to admire him, then goes into The Fission Hole;*

and DINNY *without noticing her trails after her. We are now in the play. When the three witches appear with the clock, a clear and slow ticking like that of a metronome is heard.*

The WITCHES *look like escapees from an old ladies' poorhouse.* LUELLA *is a skinny brainless thing with red hair and nose, a rush of teeth to the mouth, and a treble voice out of Brooklyn, but likable; she wears a yellow slicker and galoshes, and carries a battered old cuckoo clock.* ULGA *is a squat and unpleasant croaker with a basso voice, greenish hair, and enormous ears, but very vain; she is continually working on her looks with hand mirror, lipstick, tweezers, eyebrow pencil; she wears a torn polka-dot housedress, like a janitress, and carries a colossal directory.* ZENOBIA *is impressive, cerebral, dry and elegant, capable of rising to the grand manner when occasion offers and sometimes when it doesn't; she has jet-black hair, a chalky face, and a great hawk nose, is dressed in second-hand riches, a beaded dress and a fur piece, and carries a rusty pot with a hole in it.*

When they come in sight of the skyline, they study it.

LUELLA [BRIGHTLY]: That's the address, Zenobia.
ZENOBIA: Will you check on it, Ulga?
LUELLA: How come Ulga has to check on everything I say?
ZENOBIA: Because Ulga is efficient, Luella. You are not.
ULGA [CONSULTING HER BOOK]: It's the address, Zenobia.
ZENOBIA: Very well.

(ZENOBIA *sets the pot down on the rocks, and all*

three sit around it. They begin to prepare a brew,
snatching the ingredients out of the air, and chant-
ing.)

ZENOBIA, LUELLA, ULGA:

> *This is how the world was made,*
> *In a stew, in a stew,*
> *Toil and time and things decayed,*
> *Spit and glue, spit and glue,*
> *A pinch of malice, a pinch of man,*
> *Cook forever without a plan,*
> *This is how the world began:*
> *Stir the brew, stir the brew.*
>
> *This is how a man is mixed,*
> *In a stew, in a stew,*
> *Toadstool heart and twenty sticks,*
> *Spice with rue, spice with rue,*
> *A cup of love, a bill unpaid,*
> *A dash of soul, a key mislaid,*
> *A grain of wit, a hand grenade,*
> *Make the brew, make the brew.*
>
> *This is how the world goes round,*
> *In a stew, in a stew,*
> *Tear of angel, tooth of hound,*
> *Me and you, me and you:*
> *Sailors drown in a city puddle,*
> *Lovers part, and killers cuddle,*
> *Man, and mud, and mind, and muddle:*
> *Drink the brew.*

(They drink.)

ZENOBIA: So. Another mortal created. What's the day's count?

ULGA [CONSULTING THE BOOK]: Mortals created, three hundred twenty-five thousand seven hundred and sixty-three.

ZENOBIA: And mortals destroyed?

ULGA: Three hundred twenty-five thousand seven hundred and sixty-two.

ZENOBIA [SHARPLY]: Who's the one we missed?

ULGA: Name, Dinny Jones. Age, twenty-five. Plays trumpet in that beer joint.

LUELLA [STRICKEN]: A *musician?* What will he die of, Ulga?

ULGA [NOSE IN THE BOOK]: Decapitation.

ZENOBIA: Unusual.

LUELLA: Yes, for so young.

ULGA: Shall we take him now, Zenobia?

ZENOBIA [YAWNING]: Presently, presently.

(*She indulges in another sip of brew, and sighs.*)

I'm exhausted, all day over a hot caldron, and it's my birthday too. What time is it?

ULGA [CONSULTING THE CLOCK]: Half past the twentieth century. What's exhausted you?

LUELLA: I can't understand that clock, it's got such big spaces. And no *hands!*

(*The cuckoo pops out, and chirps cuckoo.*)

ZENOBIA: You are not expected to understand life, Luella, merely to administrate it.

ULGA: Maybe it's arteriosclerosis, how old *are* you this birthday?

ZENOBIA: That is my affair, my pot, er, pet.
LUELLA: Here, Zenobia, before it's too late. Happy
    birthday.

(*She gives her an object.*)

ZENOBIA: What is it?
LUELLA: It's a *present*.

(ZENOBIA *turns it over baffledly.*)

It's a cigar holder. With a kazoo in it, to play while
    you smoke.
ZENOBIA: That's very original, Luella.

(*And she uses it thereafter.*)

ULGA: From me.

(*She gives* ZENOBIA *a huge black spray gun labelled
with skull and bones.*)

A new kind of atomic insecticide: for people.
    Happy birthday, now can we take this Dinny—
LUELLA: What have you got against people, Ulga?
ULGA [DOURLY]: They're inefficient. Can we—
LUELLA: That's what's fun, don't you like surprises?
ZENOBIA: Please, let's have no political discussions on
    my birthday. Give me the book. I have another
    present, in here.

(*She turns the pages.*)

LUELLA: What?

ZENOBIA: An uncut page.

ULGA [INCREDULOUS]: An uncut page!

LUELLA [DELIGHTED]: An uncut page! Ooh, I'm so glad.

ULGA: It's impossible. The binder made an inefficient mistake.

ZENOBIA: It is no mistake. This page was sealed when the foundations of the earth were laid, and is to be first read on this my birthday.

(*She cuts the page.*)

LUELLA: Isn't it exciting?

ULGA: No. Zenobia, why can't we take this Dinny Jones before we—

LUELLA: But something new, something we didn't know about can happen, Ulga. What's it say?

ZENOBIA [INTONING]: "And on that day guard well the clock: lest your wits be entranced by a dream, and time slip from you: for it is written, if on that day the sorcerer come, and the clock stop, the power of the world will pass from your hands."

ZENOBIA, LUELLA, ULGA [THUNDERSTRUCK]: *What?*

(ZENOBIA *drops the book, grabs the cuckoo clock, and frantically winds it.* LUELLA *picks up the book and reads.*)

LUELLA: "If the sorcerer come, and the clock stop, the power of the world will pass from your hands???"

ULGA: I never heard anything so naïve in all my life.

LUELLA: That's a birthday present?!

ZENOBIA: Be still. Keep your wits on the clock.

(They sit huddled, and stare at it. We hear it tick-
ing, slowly and clearly, like a metronome.)

LUELLA: Seems to be running as usual.
ULGA: Certainly. Who can stop that clock? Can you?
LUELLA: No.
ULGA: No one! Who can witch a witch?
LUELLA: Not me.
ULGA: No one! Who in time can make the puniest little
    thing and say, this is out of time?
LUELLA: No one!
ULGA [ANXIOUSLY]: Is it running all right?
ZENOBIA: Yes. Keep your wits on the clock. If we only
    conclude this day's business before dawn, we will
    be safely past the danger. What was that last mor-
    tal's name?
ULGA: Dinny Jones.
ZENOBIA: Very well. Let us take him.

(She begins the chant.)

> *This is how the world will end,*
> *In a stew, in a stew,*
> *Kiss me, foe, and weep me, friend,*
> *Parting's old, parting's new—*

(The door of The Fission Hole opens, and DINNY
steps out; he carries his trumpet under his arm, his
jacket is slung over one shoulder, his necktie is
loose; he lights a cigarette, tosses the match away,
and is admiring the night sky again when behind
him the door opens and AMY, *now in a waitress's*

smock, shakes out a tableclothful of pretzels over him.)

DINNY [INDIGNANTLY]: Hey!

AMY: Oh. Scuse me, Dinny. I didn't know you were still here.

DINNY: Sure I'm still here, where do you think I'm in the, clouds? What's your name again?

AMY: Amy.

DINNY: Oh. Hiya.

AMY: You want to wait and walk me home?

DINNY: Nah, if I walk you home the first thing I know I'll be married.

AMY: Of all the conceit!

(*She goes in again, shutting the door. DINNY shouts after her.*)

DINNY: Well, I got other things to do in the world! I gotta—

(*A passage of something across the sky catches his eye; we hear it whiz.*)

Whee, look at that star shoot!

LUELLA: Poor Dinny.

ZENOBIA [VEXED]: Luella! I'll begin again.

(*She begins again.*)

This is how the world will end—

(*Pointing, DINNY runs after the star; it leads him*

around in a figure-eight, and he ends up over the
witches with his finger practically on them.)

LUELLA [LIKE PERFUME]: Good evening, Dinny.

DINNY [SCOWLING]: Evening. How come you know my
name?

LUELLA [SADLY]: It's in the book.

ZENOBIA: Luella, keep your wits on the clock!

DINNY: What've you got there?

LUELLA: A clock.

DINNY [STARING]: Is that the right time, zero?

ULGA [GLOATING]: Yes, is it later than you thought?

(DINNY *wheels from the clock sharply, scanning*
the night overhead, and pulling his collar together
as if cold.)

DINNY: Gee, I got a funny feeling. Like I'm in a dream
or something—

LUELLA: I got a funny feeling for *you*, Dinny.

ZENOBIA: Keep your wits on the clock!

ULGA: Yes, don't divide your mind, Luella, you can
hardly afford it.

LUELLA: Oh, is that so? Let me tell you something,
Ulga—

ZENOBIA: Will you *both* stop interrupting?

(*They sit quelled.*)

I'll begin again.
This is how the world will end—

DINNY: Say, what's going on here anyway? This is no
place for ladies to be having a picnic.

ZENOBIA: Picnic!

DINNY: Yeah, what do you three old— I mean, what are you doing here?

ZENOBIA [GRIMLY]: I am the main witch.

DINNY: Come again?

ZENOBIA: I make the seasons to turn, seeding and harvest, the snow to fall in the forest, the sap to rise. I make all change, and no change.

LUELLA: I'm the nit witch.

DINNY: Huh?

LUELLA: In charge of life. I make the sun to march, noon to beat, light in the east and light in the— light in the—

ULGA [IMPATIENTLY]: West!

LUELLA: West. I put the breath in the nostrils of man.

ULGA: I am the death witch. I make the moon to wheel, midnight to stand, I pull my shadow over the world. I take the breath from the mouth of man, and he grieves not.

DINNY: Okay, that's enough. Foolish question, foolish answers. Three nuts.

(*He starts to leave.*)

ZENOBIA: You nincompoop! We are the three witches who run the world!

DINNY [STOPS]: You are?

ZENOBIA: And a little more respect from you, if you please, before we run you out of it. You're only in it by a momentary oversight.

DINNY: That's a fact, my old man often said— How did you know?

ULGA [CROAKING]: Let's do away with him, Zenobia.

DINNY [QUICKLY]: I didn't mean any disrespect, I was polite as I could be.

ZENOBIA: Which leaves something to be desired. Now be on your way. We have work to do.

(DINNY *begins off, stops to ponder, looks back surreptitiously at them.*)

> This is how the world will end,
> In a stew—

(DINNY *comes back.*)

DINNY: Look, if you're who you claim to be, meaning no disrespect, it seems to me you ought to be able to give me some help.

ZENOBIA: On what?

DINNY: On something I'm looking for.

ZENOBIA: What's that?

DINNY: I don't know. Here I been in the world twenty-five years, what for? What's in it for me? I keep looking for something special, that no one else has, where is it?

ULGA [A CORRECTION]: Where *was* it.

DINNY: I don't *know*, you got wax in your ears? Only every time I see a shooting star I figure if I could just get to to where it lands, I'd find everything I'm looking for. Any of you see a shooting star land right around here just now?

ULGA [BORED]: Who would notice a star land here?

DINNY: Me! If it leads me to what I'm after. Because if I see it I'll know it, all right, I got the feeling.

ZENOBIA: Can you describe the object of this quest in *any* manner?

DINNY: Well. I can sing it, maybe, if I could sing.

LUELLA [SHUDDERING]: Ooh, please do, Dinny.

DINNY: Okay, I can.

(*He sings.*)

> *Don't know why I came here,*
> *Just followed my nose:*
> *Couldn't say what I'm after,*
> *Can't wait till it shows:*
> *Can't give you its name here,*
> *Heard it lies in my way:*
> *Don't know what I'm here for,*
> *Thought you could say.*

ZENOBIA: Not by that description, I'm afraid.

DINNY: Wait, I'll give you a clearer idea.

(*He sings again.*)

> *Don't know what I want here,*
> *Can't think what it is:*
> *Just feel like a flat beer,*
> *Need it to fizz:*
> *Didn't hear what it looked like,*
> *Hangs off there like a bell:*
> *Don't know what I'm here for,*
> *Thought you could tell.*

(*He waits a moment.*)

No?

LUELLA [SADLY]: No.

DINNY: But one of these days I'm gonna be dead, I got
to know what I'm here for first!

ZENOBIA: You raise a very profound question. But as
 you cannot put it into words, we will resume our—
DINNY: What's the good of words? Look, look, this is
 what it *feels* like.

(*He drops his jacket, and lifts the trumpet. He
 plays it, slow, lonely, tender—the preceding tune,
 but now quite sad. A cloud comes over the moon,
 except for a beam on* DINNY, *and the witches begin
 to hum along. They are interrupted by a terrific
 clap of thunder, with lightning, in the midst of
 which the metronomelike ticking stops. When the
 moon comes out again,* ZENOBIA *is gazing in horror
 at the clock. She snatches it up.*)

ZENOBIA: It's stopped!
LUELLA: Hoooo—
ZENOBIA: You idiots, you idiots! It's stopped!
ULGA: Shake it! Shake it hard!

(ZENOBIA *shakes it, to no effect.*)

LUELLA: Hoooo—
ZENOBIA: I told you! Imbeciles! I told you, keep your
 wits on the clock!
LUELLA: I kept mine on it, Zenobia.
ZENOBIA: *Yours* didn't help!
ULGA: Why didn't you keep yours on it?
ZENOBIA [GRANDLY]: I was singing, Ulga. Why didn't
 you keep yours on it?
ULGA: I was crying!
DINNY: What's all the gabble about? So the clock

stopped, wind it up again. It's no bargain as a
timepiece anyway, whyn't you get a new one?

(*They look at him, three heads like gargoyles,
turned in unison, and after a moment he backs off
a step or two.*)

ULGA: Witched by a mortal!

ZENOBIA [IN SOME FEAR]: Dinny, this is no ordinary
clock. When you made this clock stop, the power
of the world passed from us.

DINNY: When *I* made it stop?

ZENOBIA: Because this clock is Time itself!

DINNY: How did I make it stop?

ZENOBIA: I am sorry to say, your music made it stop.

DINNY: My— Let me get this straight. You mean my
horn stopped that clock?

ZENOBIA: Precisely.

DINNY [GRIMLY]: Well, how about that. I been told
off in my time, but you three buzzards are the
most. I may not be running any worlds, but one
thing, I know how to act polite.

(*He starts off again.*)

ZENOBIA [IMPERIOUS]: Dinny.

DINNY: I make a *living* at this, I'm a union member!

ZENOBIA: I believe you do not grasp the situation in its
entirety. When the power passed from our hands,
it passed to yours. You are now running the world.

(A *pause*)

DINNY [BACKING OFF]: Oh, no. No, you don't. I got
enough troubles, I gotta look for what I'm looking
for. So I'll just say so long, sorry we can't get together more often, and be—

ZENOBIA: Dinny, you have *found* what you are looking
for!

(*Comprehensively*)

The world is yours!

(DINNY *comes back, uncertain, but skeptical.*)

DINNY: You mean, this is it? It's all mine, I can have
anything I want?

ZENOBIA: Anything in the world.

DINNY [ANGRILY]: Who do you think you're pulling,
my leg?

ZENOBIA: King Dinny!

(ZENOBIA *whisks a paper crown out of the pot,
slaps it on* DINNY's *head, and the three witches
march in a ring around him, chanting.*)

ZENOBIA, LUELLA, ULGA:
   All hail, King Dinny!
   With a hey and a you and a hey you ninny
   And a hail, King Dinny!
   He won the world
   In a very odd way,
   He blew his horn
   And took it away,
   The best man won,

That's all we can say,
So hail, King Dinny!
With a hey and a you and a hey you ninny
And a hail,
Hail,
Hail,
Hail,
Hail—

(*It begins to hail, ping-pong balls, and the witches cover their heads and run about looking for shelter under tree, lamppost, and each other.*)

DINNY [SKYWARDS]: Hey, cut it out! It's August, turn off that hail!

(*The hail stops. DINNY looks around in wonder.*)

It stopped.
LUELLA [EMERGING]: Certainly. You told it to.
DINNY [DERISIVE]: Aaah. A freak of nature! Why should it stop because I—
ZENOBIA: Simpleton. Pick up a hailstone.

(DINNY *obediently picks one up, and his eyes pop.*)

DINNY: Pearls! My God, they're pearls!

(*He scrambles around, scooping them wildly into his crown.*)

ZENOBIA: Let them lie. Baubles, baubles. *Stand up!*

(DINNY *comes to attention.* ZENOBIA *makes a profound curtsy.*)

We are your servants. What are your wishes?
DINNY: You mean, anything I want I just tell you?
ZENOBIA: We are yours to command.
DINNY: How do I start?
ZENOBIA: Ascend the throne.

(*She indicates the rocks where they have been seated, which do have the semblance of a throne.* DINNY *contemplates it, then mounts it and sits.*)

Are you comfortable?

DINNY: It's a little big, but I guess I'll grow into it. What are these wires?
ZENOBIA [VICIOUSLY]: Give it to him now!

(ULGA *plunges a bicycle pump in the pot,* DINNY *leaps out just in time, the throne crackles and sizzles with blue flame.* DINNY *takes a moment to gather himself together.*)

DINNY: The hot seat! You double-crossing witch—

(*He runs at* ZENOBIA *with the horn raised as a club, she retreats around a tree, and he chases her up onto the throne, where he dares not follow.*)

ZENOBIA: Mortal, did you think the earth was to be ruled sans peur et sans reproche?
DINNY [UNCERTAIN]: I didn't think exactly *that,* but—

ZENOBIA: Come, try it again.

DINNY: Who do you think I am, out of my mind? I'm
     not sitting there till I get the first thing I want!

ZENOBIA: Name it.

DINNY [SOFTLY]: I don't want to die.

(*A pause*)

ZENOBIA: Ulga. Turn to his death.

ULGA: I don't have to turn, it's right here on page—

ZENOBIA: Tear it out.

ULGA: What?

ZENOBIA: I said, tear it out.

LUELLA [DELIGHTED]: Goody.

ULGA: But that'll upset the order of the whole uni-
     verse—

ZENOBIA [IMPATIENTLY]: We have no choice! Do as I
     instruct you.

(ULGA *endeavors to obey, but her hand will not.
She lets it drop.*)

ULGA [DISMAL]: I can't, Zenobia, it goes against the
     grain.

ZENOBIA: Then bring it here.

(ULGA *brings the book.* ZENOBIA *tears the page out,
a bright crimson one, scans it, shakes her head in
regret, crumples the page, and throws it at* DINNY'S
feet. He picks it up, weighs it in his palm.)

DINNY: I'm safe? I can't die, long as I hold onto this?

ZENOBIA: What question can there be about it?

DINNY: The question can be how do I know I can trust you!

ZENOBIA [ANOTHER CURTSY]: We are your servants.

DINNY: Yeah. Boy, have I got a servant problem. Just as soon have three rattlesnakes wash my back. All right, let's get down to business.

(*He returns to the throne, and sits gingerly.*)

Just stay away from that switch! Okay. Anything I want, huh?

ZENOBIA: Anything in the world.

DINNY [TO HIMSELF]: This is just like a dream. Now what do I want?

(*He sits pondering, opens his mouth once or twice, changes his mind, assumes a variety of thoughtful positions on the throne.* ZENOBIA *meanwhile speaks to* ULGA *as they remove their pot and things to another rock.*)

ZENOBIA [GINGERLY]: Stop sulking, we'll get it back for you in a moment.

LUELLA [HAPPILY]: No, we won't.

ZENOBIA [HISSING]: Luella, your province is life. Not eternal life. I say we—

DINNY: How much time have I got?

ZENOBIA [SWEETLY]: Aeons, aeons.

DINNY: I don't know what I want next.

LUELLA: How's about a fine bouncing wife and a good healthy—

DINNY: Wife! That's all you women think about. If I

wanted a wife I could've married whose-ye-ma-
call-it the waitress there without going through all
this!

ZENOBIA [SWEETLY]: Take your time, take your time.

DINNY: Well, as long as I got aeons, I don't have to be
a hog. Not right away. How about giving a hand
to some jerk's in a spot first, while I think over
what I really want?

ZENOBIA: If you wish.

DINNY: Yeah, I wish to be bighearted and use my power
for good. Give me somebody who's got some terrible trouble, I'll fix it up.

ZENOBIA: Give him three of your mortals.

LUELLA: Which three?

ZENOBIA: The nearest three.

LUELLA: Blow your horn!

(DINNY *blows a hot lick on the horn.*)

Look behind the rock.

DINNY [PEERS OVER]: Hey!

(A *drunk behind the rock wakes up in a hurry,
heaving himself up.*)

What's your name?

JAKE: Jake, your honor.

DINNY [MODESTLY]: Just call me King Dinny.

ZENOBIA, LUELLA, ULGA:
    All hail, King Dinny!
    With a gift and a horse and a gift horse whinny
    And a hail, King Dinny!
    He's got a load
    Of original sin,

He's going to help
A new era in,
The old error out,
A new error in,
So hail, King Dinny!
With a gift and a horse and a gift horse whinny
And a hail,
Hail—

DINNY [SKYWARDS]: Skip the hail!

(*He turns to* JAKE.)

Just kneel down a little bit, Jake, and tell me what's wrong.

JAKE [ON HIS KNEES]: I'm gonna get tired.

DINNY: In two words.

JAKE: Two words?

DINNY: Two words.

JAKE: I'm. Poor.

DINNY: No money?

JAKE: Not a goddam dime.

DINNY: How come? You got no job?

JAKE: I got a job, but I also got a wife, seven kids, a mother-in-law, two parents and an uncle to support. Just ask yourself, what if you had a wife, seven kids, a mother-in-law—

DINNY: Not me, what do you think I'm, rocks in my head? How'd you like some money?

JAKE: I think I'd like it.

DINNY: Look in that ashcan, you'll find a small bag of gold.

(JAKE *looks in the ashcan, comes up with a great*

stuffed laundry bag in his arms, and runs out.
DINNY *stares.*)

DINNY: Is that *gold?*
ZENOBIA: Naturally.
DINNY: Don't seem to weigh very much.
LUELLA: It's worth its weight in gold!
DINNY: I see. Who's next?

(AMY *has stepped out of* The Fission Hole, *which now disappears; she runs to kneel before the throne.*)

AMY: I am!
DINNY: No, stand up, ladies are different. What's your name?
AMY: Amy!
DINNY: Oh, yeah. The waitress, didn't recognize you without the apron. You need some money?
AMY [INDIGNANTLY]: No!
DINNY: Peculiar. So what do you want?
AMY: Want?
DINNY: One wish.

(AMY *closes her eyes, then speaks dreamily.*)

AMY: Money isn't what I need. I've got a treasure.
DINNY [SCOWLING]: What kind of complaint is that?
AMY: I want someone to give it to.
DINNY: Now wait a minute! I'm the one who's being bighearted here. You're supposed to be in trouble.
AMY: I am.
DINNY: Then don't be trying to give treasures away.

AMY: I—

DINNY: Just tell me what's wrong, not how much dough you've got.

AMY: I—

DINNY: Or how you're going to throw it around. All I'm interested in is your trouble, state your trouble.

(AMY *regards him with pressed lips and a lack of approval.*)

Come on, state your trouble!

AMY: I did.

DINNY: I didn't hear anything sounded like trouble.

AMY: Then whyn't you listen to a person?

DINNY: *What?*

AMY: Talk less, you might hear more.

DINNY: You know who I am, King Dinny, I could strike you dead or something?

AMY: Any way is better than you strike me now.

(*To the witches*)

Isn't that just like a man, resort to brute force if they lose an argument—

DINNY [RISING]: *Miss what's-your-name!* Now look, I've got a lot of things to settle here, all I want from—

AMY: I wonder.

DINNY: You wonder what?

AMY: If you'll settle them. You don't seem to be very— competent.

(DINNY *stands speechless a moment, then sits.*)

DINNY: I give up.

ZENOBIA: Yes, there seems to be some short circuit in communication between you. What's wrong?

DINNY AND AMY [BOTH INDIGNANT]: I can't get a word in edgewise!

LUELLA: But Dinny, you said you'd help her.

DINNY [GLOOMILY] Yeah.

(*He hisses at the witches.*)

I could use a little advice on this.

(ZENOBIA *turns a page of the book, reads, and hisses back:*)

ZENOBIA: "He that findeth his life shall lose it; and he that shall lose his life, shall find it."

DINNY [PONDERS IT, HISSES BACK]: I could use a little advice on *that*.

ZENOBIA: It states her case, obviously.

(*To* AMY)

Now as I understand what you say, this treasure is under a spell: you are forbidden access to it yourself, until you find someone to give it to, and together expend it in eternal allegiance.

AMY: Exactly.

DINNY [TAKEN ABACK]: When did she say all that?

LUELLA [WAGGING A FINGER]: Oh, we women understand each other, Dinny!

DINNY: So what does she want from me?

ZENOBIA: Directions.

LUELLA: On where to find such a person. To give it to.

DINNY: You women understand each other so good, let her get them from you.

AMY [FIRMLY]: Not directions.

LUELLA: No, you know what women's directions are! Not so hot.

DINNY: Well. You see where that black cat's going? Follow it. At the thirteenth ashcan—

AMY [OUTRAGED]: The thirteenth ashcan!

DINNY: —such a person is waiting. Personally I'm sorry for them, but that's their lookout. I'll help him out later.

AMY [WITHERINGLY]: Thank you.

DINNY [COOLLY]: Don't mention it.

(AMY *goes disgustedly out, passing a third mortal,* BEN, *who stands staring directly at* DINNY.)

Next. Step up, step up. Hey, I'm talking to you!

(BEN *is motionless.*)

Don't stand there like a dope, come here and spit it out.

(BEN *is motionless.*)

These cases are getting worse every minute. Come here!

BEN: You speaking to me?

DINNY: I said you! What are you, stupid?

BEN: No, I'm blind.

(*A pause.* DINNY *leaps down and goes up to* BEN, *to gaze in his face.*)

DINNY: How long you been blind?
BEN: I was born blind.
DINNY: You never saw any of—this?

(*He indicates the world.*)

BEN: Any of what?

(DINNY *wheels angrily on the witches.*)

DINNY: Is that the best you mildewed bats can do? Whoever told you how to run a world? If I couldn't do better with one hand tied behind me, I'd go jump in that pot!
ZENOBIA: The reality of pain is not to be circumvented, it is the necessary consequence of necessary cause, and only seems important at times.
DINNY: To me it seems important!

(*He turns to* BEN.)

What's your name?
BEN: Ben.
DINNY: Touch your eyes, Ben. Now you can see.

(BEN *opens his eyes, looks around in unbelief and joy, begins to laugh and weep. He wanders, touching at things.*)

BEN: I can see. I can see! This is a—?
DINNY: That's a tree.

BEN [SOFTLY]: A tree. And this is—?
DINNY: That's a rock.
BEN: Rocks.

(*He comes to the witches.*)

And these—?
DINNY: These are women.
BEN [IN HORROR]: Oh, no.

(*He recoils, wringing his hands, staring at them.*)

DINNY: Ben, it takes all kinds to make a world go round.
You'll see better lookers on your travels.
BEN [RECOVERING]: How can I thank you?
DINNY: Just keep your eyes open, you'll see the world.
You'll see Everything.

(BEN *kisses his hand, and goes out gazing at everything.*)

Hm. I'm gonna make some changes around here.
For everybody. First thing I'll need is all the dough
in the world.

LUELLA: Blow the horn!

(DINNY *blows;* STONEHENGE, *in a dark suit and homburg, hurries in with an oversize bankbook.*)

DINNY: Name?
STONEHENGE: Bertram Otis Stonehenge III.
DINNY: All right, B.O., just tell me how much I got
salted away in the pig.

(*He picks an apple from an overhanging tree and loafs on the throne, eating it.* STONEHENGE *opens the bankbook.*)

STONEHENGE: Two nine eight comma six eight four comma three nine—

(ULGA *fires a long pistol out of the pot at* DINNY, *but he loafs undisturbed, munching the apple.* ULGA *glares at the pistol.*)

—seven comma one two eleven comma—

ULGA [HISSING]: Not very efficient!

ZENOBIA [HISSING]: The book said decapitation, Ulga. And obviously we must have that page back.

STONEHENGE: —nine five three comma eight one four comma—

DINNY: What do you mean, comma, comma? What are you talking in, dollars, thousands, millions?

STONEHENGE: No, your highness.

DINNY [SURPRISED]: Billions?

STONEHENGE: There is no word for this amount. Three eight five comma—

DINNY [VEXED]: That's the way it always is, no word! I got to have a word, you chicks got an unused word in that book?

ZENOBIA [FLIPS A PAGE, RUNS HER FINGER DOWN]: Swillions.

DINNY: You heard her, swillions. Okay. Now get out of here in all directions and spread it around, see that everyone's taken care of with my compliments, till I can get to them personally.

STONEHENGE [STARTING]: Yes, sir.

DINNY: And hey. Put a swillion on Snail's Pace in the fifth.

STONEHENGE: I cannot recommend that investment, sir, Snail's Pace is a sure thing to come in last again.

DINNY: I know it. I'm just encouraging him.

STONEHENGE: Yes, sir.

(*He goes out.*)

DINNY: Now we're getting somewhere! Things are gonna be different, I'm making some changes. I want to see the kings of the world!

LUELLA: Blow, man!

(DINNY *blows;* TOM, DICK *and* HARRY, *in ward-heeler vests and derbies, come dancing in from opposite directions.*)

TOM, DICK, HARRY:
We are the kings of the world, of the world,
The people do not love us, we get roasted,
fried, and boiled—

DINNY [THUNDERING]: Never mind the song and dance, I got a thing or two to tell you!

TOM, DICK, HARRY [WILTING]: Yessir. Yessir.

DINNY [POINTING]: Okay. Where you from?

TOM: I am from the lost kingdom of golden towers, built of the ivory bones of slave girls, princes, and beggars.

DINNY [TAKEN ABACK]: What's the name of that place?

TOM: Atlantis. I bring you the key of the kingdom.

(*He gives* DINNY *a great key.*)

DINNY: Where you from?

DICK: I am from the lost nation of golden towers, built of the ivory bones of slave girls, princes, and beggars.

DINNY: That's the same place. What's its name this time?

DICK: Nineveh. I bring you the key of the kingdom.

(*He gives* DINNY *a great key.*)

DINNY: Where you from?

HARRY: I am from the far city of golden towers, built of the ivory bones of slave girls, princes, and beggars.

DINNY: Name of?

HARRY: Jersey City. I bring you the key of the kingdom.

(*He gives* DINNY *a great key.*)

DINNY: Thanks. If I'm near your home towns I'll stop in. Now you've been screwing everything up, you know that! That's how you two worked yourselves out of a job!

TOM, DICK: Yessir.

DINNY: I'm taking matters out of your hands, at least we still got Jersey City. See if we can't run things now a little more efficiently.

ULGA: Hah!

DINNY: There's gonna be some changes made. Soon as I figure them out.

HARRY: Yessir.

DINNY: You sit down there under that tree while I figure them out. Now we're getting somewhere!

(TOM, DICK, *and* HARRY *sit under a tree.* DINNY *speaks aside.*)

I could use a little advice on this.

(ZENOBIA *turns a page of the book, and reads aloud.*)

ZENOBIA: "Don't shoot the piano player, he's doing the best he can."

DINNY [INCREDULOUS]: Is that all you've got there?

(LUELLA *scans the book.*)

LUELLA: Here! "In the ratio of exchange between commodities, their exchange value seems independent of their use value. The common element disclosed in the exchange ratio or exchange value of the commodities is, in fact, their value. Exchange value is the necessary phenomenal form of value, the only form in which value can be expressed. For the present, however, we have to consider value in itself—"

DINNY: Wait a minute, wait a *minute!* You guys keep sitting. What's that gook mean?

(*The* WITCHES *stare at the page.* DINNY *comes and looks over their shoulders.*)

LUELLA [BRIGHTLY]: It's enema comics.

DINNY: It's what?

ZENOBIA: Economics.

DINNY: You mean to save Jersey City I got to understand all that first?

LUELLA: Hooo, that isn't the half of it! "For the present, however, we have to consider value in itself—"

DINNY: Never mind the other half! Some pretty deep stuff in that book, huh?

ULGA [DARKLY]: The secrets of the universe.

(*But* DINNY *is peering too closely;* ZENOBIA *closes the book on him, hastily. He reaches between them to the book, and tries to open it again, in vain. The* WITCHES *watch calmly.*)

DINNY: It won't open!

ZENOBIA [HAUGHTILY]: Not to mortals.

(*After a moment* DINNY *gets up, returns to the throne, looks at* TOM, DICK, *and* HARRY, *and ponders.* TOM *rises, and steals out;* DICK *rises, and follows him, not stealing out;* HARRY *rises, saunters to the throne whistling, reaches for the keys.* DINNY *knocks his hand away.*)

DINNY: Keep your hands off of them! I'll figure it out and when I do you'll hear from me. If I don't strike you dead before.

(HARRY *hurries out.* DINNY *sits gloomily.*)

Only I'm losing interest a little.

ZENOBIA [WISELY]: Yes.

DINNY: I'm getting nowhere. Maybe I need a little relaxation.

LUELLA [BRIGHTLY]: Yes.

DINNY: I'm only human, you know.

ULGA [OMINOUSLY]: Yes.

DINNY: Can't be helping other people all the time. Time comes when you have to look out for number one. I'm only human, you know.

LUELLA: Want to be a hog *now?*

DINNY: I need a little fun! I'm only human, you—

LUELLA: Blow!

(DINNY *blows; up, over, and around the rocks* DAWN, CHLOE, *and* BUBBLES *snake and slink—a blonde, raven, and redhead, garbed in various kinds of undress.*)

DAWN, CHLOE, BUBBLES [A LOW-DOWN DRAG]:
  Oh, three fun-lovers are we, are we,
  Fire, and smoke, and TNT:
  I'm a girl could use a good guy,
  Give me lovin', tell me goodbye,
  Give me gaga, googoo, gumgum, gay and
    gaudy till I could die:
  Oh, three fun-lovers are we,
  Are we.

DINNY [ROCKY]: Gog. What's your names?

DAWN: Dawn.

CHLOE: Chloe.

BUBBLES: Bub-bles.

DINNY: Gog. I mean gug. I—

(ZENOBIA *turns a page of the book, and reads aloud.*)

ZENOBIA: "If any man worship the beast and his image, and receive his mark in his forehead, the same shall drink of the wine of the wrath of God—"

DINNY [ANGRY]: Why don't you leave me alone? I'm
doing all right.

(*He crooks a finger.*)

Come and kiss me, Dawn! Now we're getting
somewhere.

(*She kisses him. He frowns; the moon dims a little,
and he looks up at it.* DAWN *sits on the throne.*
DINNY *crooks a finger.*)

Come and kiss me, Chloe!

(*She kisses him, long.* DINNY *scowls in perplexity;
the moon dims perceptibly, and he looks up at it.*
CHLOE *sits.* DINNY *crooks a finger.*)

Come and kiss me, Bubbles!

(*She thoroughly works on him. The moon dims
further;* DINNY *stares up at it, and* BUBBLES *sits.*
DINNY *turns to the witches.*)

What have you done? Why is it like nothing?
What have you done to me?

(*The moon dims out; all is black, no one is seen,
but* DINNY *is heard in fear.*)

I can't see. I can't see, the night's stuck in my eyes.
What have you done? Give me some light, why
are things going wrong? What have you done to

me, what have you done to me? Damn your black
souls, *give me some light!*

(*He blows a trumpet blast. The moon comes out
again;* DINNY *turns feverishly to embrace one of the
lovelies, and is horrified to see they have turned
into the three witches, who clutch at him, cack-
ling.*)

ZENOBIA, LUELLA, ULGA: Come and kiss me. I'm only
human, you know! Come and kiss me. I need a
little fun! Come and kiss me. Give me some googoo!

(DINNY *in terror tears himself loose, drops his horn,
plunges down from the throne, tripping and staggering, and falls to his knees by the ashcan; he
covers his face with his hands.*)

DINNY [HOARSELY]: Get away from me!
ZENOBIA [RINGINGLY]: Fool, what do you think woman
is, a bonbon?
DINNY: I made a mistake.
ULGA: Say it again.
DINNY: Everyone makes mistakes. What do you know
about what's in a man? Or what he wants?
LUELLA: One thing you want you didn't ask.
DINNY: I know.
LUELLA: So why?
DINNY: I don't know if it's real. I been looking for it, I
been looking for it, ever since I was born. I want—
I want—

(*He lifts his head: opposite,* AMY *in a wedding
gown comes wandering on, counting ashcans. The
song* DINNY *has sung earlier begins, and continues
underneath.*)

AMY: Twelve. Thirteen.

(*She sees* DINNY *by the ashcan.*)

This is the thirteenth ashcan.

(*They gaze at each other across the space, each uncertain, a little afraid.*)

DINNY: Hi.
AMY: Dinny?
DINNY: What's your name, again?
AMY: Amy.
DINNY: Mine's Dinny.
AMY: I know.
DINNY: How— how've you been, Amy?
AMY: Oh— Fine!
DINNY: I've been fine too.
AMY: Oh— Fine!
DINNY: How were the—directions?
AMY: Wonderful.
DINNY: Amy.
AMY: Dinny.
DINNY [SOULFULLY]: I think you're—*beautiful.*
AMY [SOULFULLY]: I think you're—*competent.*
DINNY: Amy.
AMY: Dinny.
DINNY: Can you cook?

AMY: Oh, can I cook!

DINNY: Can you darn socks?

AMY: I knit them! Neckties, sweaters too, I make all my
own clothes.

DINNY: Can you sing?

AMY: No. I can't sing.

DINNY [JOYOUSLY]: Who says? Listen.

(*He springs to his feet, sings.*)

> *Didn't know what I wanted,*
> *Couldn't say what I thought:*
> *Just knew I would grab it,*
> *Knew it couldn't be bought—*

AMY [SINGS, FROM THE BEGINNING]:
> *Didn't know why I came here,*
> *Wasn't sure what it meant:*
> *Didn't think I would find it,*
> *Didn't see I was sent—*

DINNY, AMY:
> *Didn't hear what you looked like,*
> *Only heard I was due:*
> *Didn't know what I'm here for,*
> *Guess it was you.*

DINNY [A PAUSE]: That means I love you, Amy.

AMY: I love you, Dinny.

DINNY: Will you—come and kiss me?

(*They meet in the center, and kiss.*)

Now we're getting somewhere! I'll love you forever, Amy, you're a *treasure.*

AMY: No, you're a treasure.

DINNY: No, you're the treasure.

AMY: No, you're the treasure.

DINNY [DARKLING]: I said you're the—

LUELLA: All right, all right, you're both treasures! Now no kidding around, love is when you're willing to push a baby carriage, right?

AMY: Right.

DINNY [WORRIED]: Right?

(LUELLA *blows a blast on his horn, and a baby carriage rolls down the path in front of them.*)

Hey! There's somebody in it!

AMY [PROUDLY]: There certainly is.

DINNY: Who is it?

AMY: It's Dinny Jones, Jr., the future of the world!

DINNY: What?

AMY: It's ours.

DINNY: Ours! Something very peculiar's going on here.

(*He circles the baby carriage, scowling.*)

ZENOBIA: You forget, you altered time into one dimension, simultaneity.

DINNY: Well yeah, but didn't you—skip something?

LUELLA: We skipped the pledge of allegiance.

DINNY: Oh well, I got aeons. Amy, I'll give you and the boy everything in the world.

AMY: I just want us to be satisfied with each other, Dinny.

DINNY: Well, certainly. Of course, I also got some work to do, them keys, for instance, I got to figure it out—

LUELLA: You going to take the pledge of allegiance?

DINNY: I am.

ZENOBIA [TO ULGA]: Now we have him!

(*She turns a page of the book, swiftly.* DINNY *kisses* AMY, *does a handspring, and ends up at the throne.*)

DINNY: Get off of my throne and summon my people, I got a speech to make.

(LUELLA *blows the horn, and* DINNY *takes it as he mounts the throne. The* WITCHES *hobble back to their pot, and the cast begins to emerge onstage.*)

Step a little closer, please. I got a thing to tell you. The story of my success!

ULGA [DARKLY]: It's not finished, yet!

DINNY [BRIGHTLY]: And it's not finished *yet!* Now here's how I got where I am. I was looking for something, special, that no one else had. I looked uptown and downtown, I looked on the east side, and I looked on the west. I didn't find it. I was feeling if I didn't find it I might as well be dead. Then I saw a shooting star. I thought it might bring me luck, if I followed it I might find what I was after. It led me here, and I won the world for a song. Everything I am today I owe to the Conn Musical Instrument Company, Elkhart, Indiana! I want to say to you—

(*He stops, lifts his head, and follows a passage of something across the sky; we hear it whiz. The* WITCHES *look up.*)

ZENOBIA: It's only a falling star.

(JAKE *wanders in, with* BUBBLES *on his arm. He is
unhappy-drunk, and trails the empty laundry bag.*)

JAKE: I'm poor. Hey, I'm poor.
DINNY: Sit down and be quiet.
JAKE: You got another bag?
DINNY: I'm making a little speech here, now sit—
JAKE [TEARFULLY]: Look, not a goddam dime. Got a
    wife, seven kids, mother-in-law, parents, uncle, and
    my *lady friend* here to support—
DINNY: Sit down and shut up!

(JAKE *collapses.*)

Lot of good I did *you.* Now I was saying—

(*He resumes, but with a lessening conviction.*)

I took over the world with this horn, it's a new day
for everyone. They said I could have anything I
could name, so I named it and had it.

(*He includes them all in a gesture, ending with*
AMY.)

Everything in the world, and you. You know what
that feels like, to get what you want? First it's like
a dream, like walking through the town and every
street lamp you pass turns into an apple tree, and
all the ashcans smell of flowers, and a cool wind
blows the newspapers out of your way. I want to
say to you—

(STONEHENGE *rushes in happily, waving fistfuls of oversize money.*)

STONEHENGE: He won, your highness! He won!

DINNY: Who won?

STONEHENGE: Snail's Pace! He won!

DINNY [INCREDULOUS]: He came in first?

STONEHENGE: First? He came in first, second, and third!

DINNY: How is that possible?

STONEHENGE: He lapped the field twice.

DINNY: How about that. I did *him* some good. Let that be a lesson to all of you, what a little encouragement can do. Now, next time he runs, we'll parlay—

STONEHENGE: Oh, he won't run again.

DINNY: Why not?

STONEHENGE [GAILY]: He burst his heart.

(*A pause.* STONEHENGE *offers him the money. Then* DINNY *puts a hand over his eyes, as though stricken, and whispers.*)

DINNY: Amy.

AMY [TROUBLED]: Dinny?

DINNY: Read the pledge.

LUELLA [WITH THE BOOK]: "Whither thou goest, I will go; and where thou lodgest, I will lodge; thy people shall be my people, and thy God my God: where thou diest, will I die, and there will I be buried."

(To AMY)

Swear.

AMY: I do.

LUELLA [TO DINNY]: Swear.

ZENOBIA [TO ULGA]: If he but swears—

(DINNY *lifts his head, and follows a passage of something across the sky; we hear it whiz. The* WITCHES *look up.*)

ULGA: It's only a falling star.

DINNY: I want to say to you—

(BEN *enters. He stands and gazes past* DINNY.)

BEN: The things I've seen. I walked on the east side, and I walked on the west. My eyes were open, and I saw the world. I saw Everything, behind us and ahead. I want one thing.

DINNY: Name it.

BEN: I want my blindness back.

(*Long pause*)

ZENOBIA [TO DINNY]: "Where thou diest, will I die, and there will I be buried." Swear.

DINNY [VERY UNCERTAINLY]: I was saying. You get what you want. And something— Something goes wrong inside. A cold wind blows the newspapers. It blows the street lamps down. It blows the ashes in the air, the wind is a mouthful of ashes. Something goes wrong inside, why does it go wrong? You get everything you want, and something else is calling your name. What do you know of what's in a man? Or what he wants. Or what he wants!

(*He screams at the* WITCHES.)

What have you done to me?

ZENOBIA: Given you everything in the world. Swear.

(DINNY *stands rigid, then turns to* BEN.)

DINNY: What did you see, ahead?

BEN: I saw how the world—turns, like a skull. I saw the
grass die and the grasshopper, dog eating dog and
vomiting—death, I saw—Death. In the atom, and
everything under the sun.

DINNY: Amy even? The boy even? What if I touch
them, and say live?

BEN: I saw everything you touch, cry.

(DINNY *covers his face. After a while he whispers:*)

DINNY: No. Once, once before I die, I want—something
that—won't spoil, won't turn crooked on me, won't
—go wrong—

ZENOBIA: You want something perfect.

DINNY: Once.

ZENOBIA: Perfection is not in the world.

(DINNY *lifts his head, and follows a passage of
something across the sky; we hear it whiz. The*
WITCHES *look up.*)

LUELLA: It's only a falling star.

DINNY [WATCHING]: Which way are they falling?

ULGA: South.

LUELLA: North.

ZENOBIA: East by west. "Where thou diest, will I die."
Swear!

(DINNY *looks down again.*)

DINNY: I want to say to you—

(*He pauses, gazes around.*)

—so long.

(*He picks up the keys, and descends from the throne. He distributes the keys among the people, one to* BEN, *one to* JAKE, *one to the baby.* DINNY *then picks up his jacket and horn, and climbs the path to leave.* AMY's *voice catches him.*)

AMY: Dinny! You said I'd find—such a person—
DINNY: I couldn't even give you the right directions. I'm not the person.
AMY: But I love you, Dinny.
DINNY: Amy, nothing turns out right in the end, how can I swear to us?
AMY: Won't you at least try?
DINNY: I'm afraid to touch you, how can I swear to die when everything I touch goes bad, like in a bad dream, and I don't know why?
ZENOBIA: Original sin.
ULGA: Inefficiency.
LUELLA: Human nature.
DINNY [A PAUSE]: I just didn't know.

(*As though to himself, he half talks the song:*)

> Didn't know what I wanted,
> Couldn't say what I thought:
> Just know that we're put here,
> Just know that we're caught,
> Just know that we're haunted,
> Stars fall, like bells:
> Didn't know what I wanted,
> But something else.

(He stands a moment, the song continuing under; then he turns, and goes up the path and out. The people drift slowly off, one pushing the baby carriage. AMY and the WITCHES remain, AMY looking after DINNY.)

AMY: Which way is he going?

(The WITCHES are silent.)

Will he find it?

(No reply. She reaches out her hand behind her.)

Look in the book.

(The WITCHES shake their heads.)

Dinny.

(She puts her hand over her mouth. Then she too goes off slowly, opposite from DINNY.)

ULGA: But he still has the page!

LUELLA: Yes, isn't he lucky?

ZENOBIA [OUTRAGED]: Lucky! That man is dangerous: every breath he draws is a threat to the status quo!

LUELLA: What's that?

ZENOBIA, ULGA: Us!

ZENOBIA: He must swear to die, for something. One of us will follow him, cast an irresistible spell of involvement around him—

LUELLA [EAGERLY]: I'll go!

ZENOBIA: No, he'll cast a spell around you. Ulga, after him! Luella, after that girl.

(LUELLA *trots out after* AMY; ULGA *lopes after* DINNY.)

We'll trap him with her!

(ZENOBIA *rises to her full height above the caldron, and prays down to it, in ringing voice.*)

Father in hell, forgive us our trespasses. Give us this night our human blood. Thy kingdom, come! give us temptation and evil, deliver him up to us! Let no man escape: or theirs is the kingdom, the power, and the glory forever.

(*With a gesture she blacks out the moon, and the curtain falls.*)

ACT II

IT IS STILL NIGHT IN THE PARK.

The scene is now a shambles. The street lamp is collapsing, the park bench has rotted, and all the trees are as dead as stone. Half the skyline buildings are in ruins. The Fission Hole door is padlocked, bears a lopsided old sign, "CLOSED," and is matted by a huge cobweb; the cobweb bears a tiny sign. In the moonlight on top of the rocks is a statue veiled in a moth-eaten sheet.

And the people are in rags, of their former costumes. There is a mass meeting in progress: ZENOBIA, on a ladder topped with a skull-and-bones flag, is haranguing the cast in a ring around her, all present but DINNY and AMY; among them JAKE bears a placard reading, "Give the Bankers Home Relief, We Want Jobs," and STONE-HENGE opposite bears another reading, "Give the Home Reliefers Banks, We Want Jobs."

They are booing and heckling ZENOBIA, who is a little desperate.

ZENOBIA: And in conclusion I will be brief.

(*Cheers, derisive cries of thanks.*)

Looking backward on the five thousand years of this administration, what do we find? Peace, prosperity, social progress— Eek!

(*The ladder gives way;* ULGA *and* LUELLA *grab it, holding her up.*)

LUELLA [BRIGHTLY]: The ladder's rotting, too!
TOM [BELLIGERENTLY]: What about all these complaints on what's happening?

(*He waves a portfolio bursting with telegrams.*)

ZENOBIA: But you are all invited to the wedding, what more do you want?
DAWN: We want to know, what's happening?
LUELLA: Just a little wedding!
ZENOBIA: Yes, the world's wedding!
ULGA: Nothing's happening. The clock is stopped.
HARRY: That's the trouble, *nothing's happening!*
CHLOE: Here it's a hundred years now, honey, nothing's happened!
ZENOBIA: Nonsense, how can you tell it's a hundred years when the clock is stopped? But we have a trap in mind—
BEN: All the clocks have stopped.
DICK: We know it's a hundred years by the things that *haven't* happened!
HARRY: We've missed five wars, that's a hundred years!
ZENOBIA: We have a number of traps in mind—
STONEHENGE [TOPPING HER]: Paralysis, everywhere! I had it all sewed up, Wall and Broad Street in my back pocket, suddenly the bottom dropped out!
BUBBLES: Is this town dead, brother!
TOM: Steel hasn't made a dollar in a hundred years, they don't like that.

HARRY: Oil, the same story, they say the next barrel they get they're gonna cook us in it.

DICK: Lead too, they keep asking us why we don't get the lead out!

DAWN: Everybody's starving!

STONEHENGE: Even the people are starving.

JAKE [DRUNK]: I'm thirsty!

TOM: Yes, the people are kicking too. Small things, but—

DICK: Read her a couple.

(TOM *pulls a telegram at random from the portfolio, while* ZENOBIA *makes a final valiant effort to stave it off.*)

ZENOBIA: Looking backward on the five thousand traps of this administration—

TOM [TOPPING HER]: Here's Maggie Callahan, wires us she's been having a baby for the last hundred years—

HARRY: Is that fair? Little fella gets born, on his first birthday he's a hundred and one years old?

ZENOBIA: Luella.

(LUELLA *files it in her bosom.*)

DICK [ANOTHER TELEGRAM]: Here's Billy Addlewitz, in the third grade for a hundred years, mother wants to know why. Thinks it's the teacher's fault.

ZENOBIA: Ulga.

(ULGA *files it in her bosom.*)

TOM [ANOTHER]: Here's Oscar Dibble, his mother-in-law's been in the bathroom a hundred years now, he wants her out.

ZENOBIA: Why?

HARRY [ANOTHER]: Here's— Oh? One for you.

ZENOBIA: A telegram for me, how charming.

HARRY [HANDS IT UP]: It's in blood.

ZENOBIA [READING]: *"What on earth is going on, on earth? Poppa!"*

(*The* WITCHES *are shattered; the ladder and* ZENO-BIA *get dropped out of sight, while* LUELLA *and* ULGA *run around in a panic and take cover.*)

LUELLA [TREMBLING]: Hooo—

ULGA [TREMBLING]: If Poppa's on another rampage—

ZENOBIA: Don't say it, Ulga.

(*She rises again on the ladder, imperious.*)

This mad fiend Dinny with his insane lust for power must go! Our directives were to expunge him next: when we do, the clocks and the world will start again!

STONEHENGE: Then expunge him!

ZENOBIA: Impossible, while he *wants* to live. He has the page his death is written on.

TOM: Well, if *we* get our hands on him, he won't want to live!

BUBBLES: Yeah, let the boys talk him around!

HARRY: Give him to us, he won't want to live!

ZENOBIA: Force is useless against that page. He must

marry the world, for better or worse! Remember, more flies with honey!

DICK: What honey?

ZENOBIA: A perfect world. In the form of Woman!

(She snatches the sheet off the statue. It is AMY *in her wedding gown with her hand on the baby carriage, looking like white marble in the moonlight.)*

He weds this world and they live happily ever after, except for one thing, her immediate demise. Then his.

(Cheers)

Are we united?

ALL [NOT BEN OR JAKE]: Yes!

ZENOBIA: Then, to work! Ulga, what kind of spell did you employ? Ulga!

(She glares around, and ULGA *reappears between legs.)*

ULGA: I shot a star across his nose. I've got him following it around Columbus Circle in a circle.

ZENOBIA: Very efficient. Now. Identify her with that plaque, Luella. Bring the star this way, Ulga.

*(*LUELLA *gets a plaque from the pot,* ULGA *summons a star.)*

And clap the trap! Once he gives back the world and that page—

ULGA: Off with his head!

(*Cheers from the* MORTALS)

LUELLA [MILDLY]: It didn't say *that* in the book.
ULGA: It did.
LUELLA: It didn't.
ULGA: Did.
LUELLA: Didn't.
ULGA: Did!
LUELLA: Didn't!
ZENOBIA: Luella, it said decapitation.
LUELLA [TRIUMPHANT]: Well?
ZENOBIA: That means, off with his head!
LUELLA [DISMAYED]: Is *that* what it means?
ULGA: What did you think it meant?
LUELLA: I thought it meant old age. When you get old
    and de—decapit?

(*She is so undermined she gropes her way downstage to sit, apart; the others are stunned.*)

STONEHENGE: One thing we can't understand is why
    the strings of life were put in *her* hands.
BUBBLES: They snafu her!
DICK: Makes for snafusion all around!
ZENOBIA: Yes, it's just like some tale told by an idiot or
    something.
LUELLA [HER FEELINGS HURT]: Owww—
ZENOBIA: Nevertheless, duty calls! Clap, trap!
LUELLA: What clap, trap?
ZENOBIA: Clap, traps within traps.

LUELLA [INDIGNANT]: I'm not going to trap him. A *musician?!*

ZENOBIA: You will do as decreed, Luella. Now, let us pray.

(*She intones:*)

O the world will wash its hands again in gore and love and fraud—

ALL: Mend and wreck—

LUELLA: Mend and wreck—

ZENOBIA: For mine eyes have seen the glory of the coming of the sword—

ALL: On his neck—

LUELLA: On his—neck?

ZENOBIA: And the worms shall sing his praises when he is their bed and board—

ALL: Leaving not a speck—

LUELLA [HORRIFIED]: Not a *speck?*

ZENOBIA: While we go marching on. Come, friends, I will explain your part in the trap. Make ready for the bridegroom!

(*She sweeps out, leading all after her except LU-ELLA, seated with her face in her hands, and JAKE and BEN; each still has his great key to the kingdom. BEN then starts off in the opposite direction.*)

JAKE: Where you going, Ben?

BEN [A PAUSE]: To open *his* eyes. If I have to.

JAKE [PUZZLED]: Why'd he give *us* the keys?

(*He goes off after BEN, leaving LUELLA alone,*

sniffling. She wipes her eyes, gets up to follow
ZENOBIA, *then turns back to speak to the audi-*
ence.)

LUELLA [MOURNFULLY]: Maybe I'm an idiot, and maybe
I'm not so bright either, but one thing I'm always
in favor of, is the next breath. You can't take that
away from me. No, sir. I know things go wrong
sometimes, I do my best but so much is going on,
in China, and Iceland, and Jersey City, it's very
hard to keep track. But I see how people feel
when they're blue. I wish I could tell them sometimes, like right now, if I could get them all together, I'd tell them, so, what if you're blue?
Don't give up so easy, I'll get it straightened out.
Probably. I always say, take the next breath.
But how can he breathe, without his head? I don't
see how. I thought it was old age, now I'm blue
myself. I wish I was dead, instead of him.

(*She cries, and blows her nose.*)

ZENOBIA [OFF]: Luelllllllah!

(LUELLA *trots woefully off. The stage is empty,*
except for the baby carriage and AMY *in the*
moonlight.

Offstage a song begins, faint as wind in the trees,
a dark song. After a moment we hear a familiar
whiz, and then DINNY'S *voice, weary and hope-*
less.)

DINNY: Whee, look at that star shoot.

(He comes trudging on with his horn, finger aloft, following his star, but so worn out his feet plod and his eyes are almost closed; he is also in rags. The finger takes him to the night-club threshold, where he halts, waiting, and finally it dawns on him where he is.)

Can't be right. What am I doing here?

(He looks around, reaches through the cobweb to try the padlocked door, shouts in.)

Hey!

(He sees the lopsided sign, and reads it in an upper-case voice.)

"CLOSED."

(Now he sees the tiny sign on the cobweb, lifts it with a finger, reads it in a lower-case squeak.)

"closed."

(He turns around, taking in the desolate scene, but AMY *is just any statue.)*

Gee, I got a funny feeling. Like I'm in a nightmare or something.

(He finds himself at the collapsing street lamp, and straightens it; it sags again when he lets it go, to gaze around.)

Something I don't remember, what is it? Somewhere, I left something, somewhere. I—

*(He talks his way slowly into the dark song, as
though hearing the words on the wind:)*

> I turned my back, and a fog
> Came round me—

AMY [ECHOING]:
> I couldn't get back, and nightfall
> Bound me
> Away—

(DINNY frowns.)

DINNY:
> Till the day
> I will come
> To a house where she is dumb—

(He is at the Fission Hole entrance.)

> I talk to her now, and my love
> Can't get in—

AMY:
> The doors are locked, and the windows
> Let in
> No light—

DINNY: Funny type echo around here.

*(He looks around, bangs his ear, picks up the
song at its bridge:)*

> I come back, but the fog's
> At my feet—

AMY:

> And my echo's the one thing
> I meet—

(DINNY *turns, and sees the statue; he is staggered. Making his way to it, he points and stammers.*)

DINNY: What, what it—it looks—it's like—looks just like—Amy!

(*The* WITCHES *now sweep in upon him; they bear top hat, swallowtail, cravat, spats, and other appurtenances which they clap on him in a dazzling performance of chant and dance:*)

ZENOBIA, LUELLA, ULGA:

> Why, hail! It's Dinny!
> O the ig and the no and ig no miny
> Of rags, on Dinny!
> Bring a tall top hat
> For the well-dressed groom,
> And a perfect cravat,
> And a flower in bloom,
> And a spit, er, spat,
> And tails for his tomb,
> And a fare, well Dinny!
> With a gold and a stick and a gold
>   stick pinny
> And a hail,
> Hail—

(But DINNY *manages to break away from them, staggering back toward* AMY.)

DINNY: Who is that statue?!
ZENOBIA: There is a plaque on it which tells who it is.
DINNY [READING THE PLAQUE]: "General Sherman"???
ZENOBIA [FURIOUS]: Luella!
LUELLA [FLUSTERED]: I got the wrong plaque!

(She flies to remove it; ZENOBIA *flies to the pot for another, and forward-passes it to* ULGA *behind* DINNY'S *back;* ULGA *lays it at* AMY'S *feet, then comes to the pot and lifts out a huge butcher's cleaver.)*

DINNY [MEANWHILE]: But it looks just like what's-her-name, the girl I left behind!
LUELLA: So why did you?
DINNY: I was afraid, Luella—
ZENOBIA: Yes, he tried the ways of the world, and with its material as is, found nothing incorruptible.
ULGA: But what if it was—

(Testing the cleaver with her thumb)

—perfect!
DINNY [RECKLESSLY]: If it was perfect, I'd take a chance!

*(*STONEHENGE *enters with a large bouquet.)*

Why did they put up this statue to her?
ZENOBIA: Read the plaque.

DINNY [READING]: "Shooting Star. The Perfect Woman."

(STONEHENGE *lays the bouquet at* AMY's *feet, and kneels in prayer.*)

ZENOBIA: The one thing you have sought. Perfection! The world as Woman, waiting to be wed!

DINNY: You mean it was right under my nose?

ZENOBIA: Precisely.

DINNY: Where is she, where can I find her? Luella, help me find her and I'll—

(*He runs to* LUELLA, *but* ZENOBIA *intervenes.*)

ZENOBIA: I will help you. But first, are you worthy of her?

DINNY: What do you mean?

ZENOBIA: Are you The Perfect Man?

DINNY: You mean am I a plastic saint or something?

ZENOBIA: No, I mean a real saint, like Paul of Tarsus, Thomas Aquinas, and T. S. Eliot? Oh, I know you've outgrown all the material temptations, but—

(*She sniffs.*)

—you do still have a smell of the world about you somewhere—

STONEHENGE [STILL KNEELING]: I noticed it too. Neglects himself under the—

ZENOBIA: Speak when spoken to, Stonehenge.

(STONEHENGE *returns to prayer.*)

It emanates from your hip pocket, what can it be?

(DINNY *feels in his pocket, brings out the crumpled page.*)

That page!

DINNY: Yeah, this is that page that tells when I'll die.

ZENOBIA: Well, to wed this ideal world, you should rid yourself of it.

DINNY: I should?

ZENOBIA: Oh, yes.

LUELLA [A MOUSE SQUEAK]: Don't.

(ZENOBIA *glares at her.*)

I didn't say anything.

ZENOBIA: Dinny, just as you desire perfection in your world, so we desire perfection in ours. Our interests are identical, you see.

DINNY: I see.

ZENOBIA: But our book, which contains all the secrets of the universe, is incomplete without that page. Now what I propose is a simple exchange, we give you a perfect world, you give us back the imperfect one and that page. Fair enough?

DINNY [UNCERTAIN]: It *seems* fair enough—

LUELLA [ANOTHER SQUEAK]: Don't.

(ZENOBIA *and* ULGA *glare at her.*)

I didn't say anything!

DINNY: —only are you sure this time you can manage it without getting it turned inside out on me?

ZENOBIA [FRIGIDLY]: Really. You read the plaque. Return the world and the page, and this statue of perfection, this same statue, accept no substitutes, I will give this very statue breath—

(*Behind her hand to* ULGA)

—temporarily—and you will live wedded to perfection for the rest of your, hmm, hmm, natural life.

DINNY [WORRIED]: But this page is a sure thing—

ZENOBIA: Dinny. What we offer instead is without mortal precedent, perfection, bliss, the ecstasy of pure spirit, without spot or spat, bodiless, a world out of this world, the attainment of Nirvana!

DINNY [IMPRESSED]: Gee.

(*He takes a breath.*)

Okay. Here's the only—

LUELLA [IN ANGUISH]: Dinny, don't you give her that page!

DINNY: What?

(ZENOBIA *and* ULGA *with the cleaver converge menacingly upon* LUELLA.)

ZENOBIA, ULGA: Luella—

LUELLA [BACKING OFF]: I didn't say a word!

DINNY: Here's the only question, how do I know I can trust you? I'll make *you* an offer.

(*He tears the page in two;* ULGA *and* ZENOBIA *swing back, horrified.*)

ULGA: Don't tear it up!

DINNY: Half down, half on delivery.

ZENOBIA: What, petty bargaining?

DINNY: Half down, half on delivery.

ZENOBIA: What kind of saintly perfectionist cares about *half* an ephemeral thing like life?

DINNY: Half down, half on delivery.

ZENOBIA [OUTRAGED]: Do you think I have no sense of personal dignity?

DINNY: Take it or leave it.

ZENOBIA: I'll take it.

DINNY: It's a deal.

ZENOBIA: Half the world and page now, half later.

(DINNY *gives her one half, pockets the other.*)

Let the wedding begin!

STONEHENGE: Yes, sir.

(STONEHENGE *rises, gets out a portable old-fashioned victrola, and winds it up.* LUELLA *snatches a whisk broom from the pot, and tidies up* DINNY. ULGA *watches her suspiciously.*)

ULGA: Zenobia. Psst!

(ZENOBIA *joins* ULGA, *who leads her downstage; they stop when they hear* LUELLA *speak approvingly to* DINNY.)

LUELLA: Half a life is better than none!

ULGA: Zenobia, I don't trust Luella. I think she's losing her nerve. I'm not even sure she's in with us now.

ZENOBIA: What? Surely you don't think she's gone over to the side of the angels?

ULGA: No, not that far. But *mortals*. She's with them too much, you know what I mean?

ZENOBIA: Her work requires it.

ULGA: That's what *she* says. The way she acts about this Dinny, I think she's—falling in love with him.

ZENOBIA: But we cannot fall in love.

ULGA: That's what I mean. I hate to say this, but I think—I think—

ZENOBIA: Yes?

ULGA: —she's becoming part human herself.

ZENOBIA [ENRAGED]: Ulga! Don't be vulga. How dare you say such a thing, and about your own sister?

(*The victrola has begun to play, a wheezy wedding march.*)

Now keep your head, and leave his to me. Places, please!

(*The* WITCHES *gather to sit at their pot,* ULGA *sulking;* DINNY *mounts the rock on the other side of the baby carriage from* AMY, STONEHENGE *takes up a lower elevation with the* WITCHES' *book in his hands, and from the wings a processional—of* DAWN, CHLOE, *and* BUBBLES *from one side, and of* TOM, DICK, *and* HARRY *from the other—enters, to the march, all strewing flower petals.*)

DAWN, CHLOE, BUBBLES [CHANT]:
            Here's to the world—
ZENOBIA, LUELLA, ULGA [CHANT]: Yes!

DAWN, CHLOE, BUBBLES:
>   *Half baked and boiled—*

(*The* WITCHES *exchange frowns.*)

>   *Witch watched*
>   *And mitch motched,*
>   *Spell bound and spoiled—*

ZENOBIA: No, no—

TOM, DICK, HARRY [CHANT]:
>   *Here's to her mate—*

ZENOBIA, LUELLA, ULGA [CHANT]: Yes!

TOM, DICK, HARRY:
>   *Blind on a date*
>   *With rack of*
>   *Love, back of*
>   *Ball number eight—*

ZENOBIA, ULGA: No, no!

STONEHENGE [CHANT]:
>   *Here's to their choice—*

ZENOBIA, LUELLA, ULGA [CHANT]: Yes!

STONEHENGE:
>   *Badder or worse,*
>   *Both in a*
>   *Trice win a*
>   *Trip in a hearse—*

DINNY: Huh?

ZENOBIA: No, no, no!

LUELLA: It's getting out of hand again—

ULGA: People!

ZENOBIA: Don't improvise, get to the pledge!

ULGA [BRANDISHING THE SPRAY GUN]: If they give the

whole trap away, I'll use the atomic insecticide on them—

ZENOBIA: Read the pledge, just read the old sweet pledge!

STONEHENGE: Certainly, sir. Kneel.

(The six kneel, and STONEHENGE *addresses* DINNY:)

STONEHENGE: Repeat after me. "I pledge allegiance to the flag—"

ALL: "—and to the republic for which it stands, one nation—"

ZENOBIA: Not that one! In the book, will you simply open the book and read?

STONEHENGE: Yes, *sir.*

ULGA: How I hate people! Can't count on them for—

(STONEHENGE *endeavors to open the book, in vain.*)

STONEHENGE [HELPLESSLY]: I can't, sir.

ZENOBIA [RISING, IRATE]: Madam! Madam!

DAWN [BOUNCING UP]: Yes?

CHLOE: Not you, honey.

ZENOBIA: Kneel down!

DAWN: Someone paged me!

ZENOBIA: No one paged anyone, the only page on *my* mind is the one from this book which—

(*—and turning en route to the book falls over* TOM, *who is on his knees in her path, searching.*)

What are you *doing?*

TOM: I'm looking for a stud.

ZENOBIA: Looking for a stud!

TOM: It's part of the ceremony, isn't it?

BUBBLES: Boy, you're not the only one, another hundred years like this and you could fry an egg on me—

ZENOBIA: Quiet!

HARRY: Is that a way to talk to this vision of loveliness?

ZENOBIA: What!

STONEHENGE [TO DINNY]: You have the ring?

DINNY: What ring?

DAWN [KNEELING AGAIN]: I distinctly heard someone paging me—

DICK: Yeah, first you insult this kid with false accusations and—

ZENOBIA: Who?

DICK: You!

ZENOBIA: What false accusations?

DICK: Madam!

STONEHENGE: Madam!

DAWN [BOUNCING UP]: Yes?

STONEHENGE: He forgot the ring, sir!

ZENOBIA [ERUPTING]: QUIET!

(*All freeze, in a total silence.*)

DINNY [WORRIED]: Don't seem to be very perfect, so far.

ZENOBIA: Yes, you can see the shoddy material we have to work through! No wonder none of you has the strength of character to open the book. Here!

(*But when she takes it from* STONEHENGE *and tries, she cannot either. She glares at it in consternation, tries again, and fails.*)

Ulga!

(ULGA *comes running; she skids her cleaver down behind the rock, and they endeavor to pry the book open, but fail.*)

ULGA: Luella!

(LUELLA *comes running; the three of them struggle over it together, to no avail.*)

LUELLA [BRIGHTLY]: It's stuck.
DINNY: Is anything going wrong?
ZENOBIA [HAUGHTILY]: Wrong? Certainly not.

(*They lay the book down,* ULGA *standing on its lower cover,* ZENOBIA *and* LUELLA *tugging at its upper.*)

DINNY: I thought maybe something was going wrong—
ZENOBIA [PANTING]: Not at all, we run nothing if not a well-ordered world, the right thing in the right place at the right time, we never deviate from that rule. Don't lack confidence.
DINNY [STRIPPING HIS WEDDING GARB]: Oh, it isn't that I don't lack confidence. I just better get out of here, though, while I got half a—

(*He clambers down the rocks, and* ZENOBIA *leaving the book darts over to grab his sleeve.*)

ZENOBIA: What, abandon her at the altar, you cad?

DINNY [HAPPILY]: But I forgot the ring! I'll just run
down to Tiffany's and pick up a—
ZENOBIA [AT LARGE]: Make him a ring!

(*The mortals make a ring around him.*)

Lead him to the slaughter— Altar!

(*The mortals lift* DINNY, *and bear him back to the
rocks.*)

DINNY: Hey! Hey, let me— Put me down, you—

(*They put him down, on the rock, but struggling;
they suppress him by piling on, and* DINNY *ends up
on his back with his head hanging over, upside
down, all sitting on him.*)

ZENOBIA: We'll step up the wedding service a bit, I
have it by memory. Do you take this world for
your lawful wedded world, forsaking all others, to
love and to cherish, in sickness and in health, for
better or worse, till death do you join? Swear.
DINNY [STRANGLING]: Get this mob offa me—
ZENOBIA: They are only witnesses, every groom feels
the same. Thy people shall be my people, where
thou diest will I die and there will I be buried?
Swear.

(DINNY *gives out with a death croak.*)

Let him swear.

(*The mortals slide off,* DINNY *lies gasping.*)

DINNY: Goddammit.
ZENOBIA: And there will I be buried?

(DINNY *takes a swallowful of air.*)

Swear!
DINNY [ON HIS BACK]: I'm not marrying no statue, and
that's final! Who do you think I am, ridiculous?
ZENOBIA: But we made a deal!
DINNY [ROLLING OVER, UP ON HIS KNEES]: Sure we did,
for a perfect woman! You call this hunk of crock-
ery a woman?
ZENOBIA: I will make it a woman!
DINNY: I said a *perfect* woman!
ZENOBIA: I said a perfect woman, whose idea was it in
the first place?

(*She swings into a huddle with* LUELLA *and* ULGA,
hissing:)

I think he's beginning to resist!
ULGA: We *say* we're giving it to him, then we get that
half page back, then we *give* it to him! What can
we lose?
ZENOBIA: Perfect!
DINNY [CALLING]: How'll I know she's perfect?
ZENOBIA: You will *hear* me. We shall call forth all her
mortal vices. Come, girls.

(*She leads* LUELLA *and* ULGA *back to the pot.* LU-
ELLA *protests in a whisper.*)

LUELLA: Zenobia, what are you trying to do? You know
we can't change human nature.

ULGA: Every change is an improvement, isn't it?

LUELLA: Certainly! only every improvement is for the
worse. Now we better be careful—

ZENOBIA [TO DINNY]: Simply maintain that posture,
while I call forth the seven sins.

LUELLA: Zenobia, be careful—

ZENOBIA: Abra, cadaver, savoir, vivre.

LUELLA: Don't—

ZENOBIA: Sloth, come forth!

LUELLA: Watch your step—

ZENOBIA: Likewise envy, gluttony, lust, anger, pride,
avarice, etcetera.

LUELLA [TREMBLING]: Hooo—

ZENOBIA: There! I have called forth every sin! She is
humanity, at its purest!

(*She rises, with a clap of her hands at* AMY; DINNY
turns around, as AMY *stirs and gazes upon him.*)

DINNY [JOYOUSLY]: Amy, it's you!

ZENOBIA: Now swear!—upon that page. I do! Swear!

DINNY [TAKING AMY'S HAND]: I—

(*Violent thunder and lightning. The entire night
sky turns red above the park; all its objects begin
to shift and swim in a lurid red smolder. The*
WITCHES' *heads crane heavenwards.*)

ZENOBIA: What on earth—

(AMY *emits an unearthly wail like a siren, which*

*blends into a wailing burst of dirty music from the
night-club, founded on an ostinato bass of "We
are the kings of the world, of the world"; this bass
persists until further notice, with the other tunes
riding in and out over it.* AMY *dances gleefully out
of* DINNY's *hand, down the rocks, unzipping her
wedding gown.)*

DINNY: Amy—

(AMY *stepping out of the gown dances wickedly
for herself.)*

DINNY: Amy!

(LUELLA *snatches up the wedding gown, to bring
it to* AMY.)

LUELLA: Amy! She said pure-est, not bare-essed!

(AMY *slaps her away, and shrieks at large:)*

AMY: Bring me my animals! I need some woo pitched!
    Bring me my horses!
DINNY [DIZZILY]: What's that?!
AMY [SCREAMING]: Bring me my horses! Bring me my
    elephants! I need some woo!

(*She pounces on* TOM, DICK, HARRY.)

    You'll do!
TOM [SURPRISED]: We'll do?
HARRY: Need a little fun fun?

DICK: I'm only human, you know! Lusty lusty!
ALL: Lusty lusty!

(AMY *pulls the three of them happily prancing back around the rocks, and they sink out of sight.*)

DINNY [REELING]: Amy!

(*He climbs on top of the rocks, peers over.*)

Amy!

(*He turns back in consternation to the witches.*)

What'd you do, turn her into a *hop*-head?
AMY [BEHIND THE ROCK]: Give me gaga, googoo, gum-gum, gay and gaudy till I *drop* dead—
DINNY: But Amy! You said you couldn't sing—

(*The witches hold a hurried consultation of dismayed faces.*)

ULGA: What *did* you do?
ZENOBIA: I haven't the faintest!
LUELLA [BEWILDERED]: Lusty lusty, what happened to lovely lovely?

(DINNY *grabs up his horn, like a club.*)

DINNY: I'm coming down!
STONEHENGE [DETAINING HIM]: By the way, I have your final bank statement.

(*He produces the oversize bankbook; it is stamped with great holes.*)

Cancelled.

(DINNY *glares at him, and jumps out of sight.* STONEHENGE *takes hold of the baby carriage, calls down to him over the rocks.*)

I'm sorry, I must foreclose on this now.

(*He lowers the carriage bumpily down the rocks.* DINNY *at once reappears around the other side, pursued by* AMY, *in her bra and panties, and brandishing* ULGA'S *cleaver.*)

AMY: Let me at him, let me at him! I'll kill him, the double-crossing son of a witchy washy flutter mucking blasted—

(*The witches drop the book, horrified, and* ZENOBIA *covers her ears.*)

DINNY [DESPERATELY]: All I said is we're practically married, why so angry?
AMY: Who's angry?

(*She swings at* DINNY'S *head, he ducks under the cleaver, and* LUELLA *intervenes to catch* AMY'S *wrist.*)

LUELLA: You're angry, I know anger when I see it—

(*Staggered:*)

It's Anger!

(AMY *swings at her,* LUELLA *ducks, and the weight of the cleaver carries* AMY *reeling off into the midst of* DAWN, CHLOE, *and* BUBBLES, *who sit her on a rock;* AMY *at once crosses one leg serenely, and using the peg hole of the cleaver as a lorgnette, speaks with dripping elegance.*)

AMY: That's rather a handsome creation.

LUELLA: Oh my goodness, it's Pride, they're coming out like bedbugs!

DAWN [MODELLING HER RAGS]: I'm proud you like it. It's an Oak Ridge original.

AMY: I make all my own clothes, it's a matter of pride—

ZENOBIA, ULGA [AGHAST]: Pride!

AMY: —but you can see I simply haven't a thing to wear tonight, and here we are on the very eve of the fall out-season. *That's* rather a handsome creation.

BUBBLES [MODELLING HER RAGS]: Oh, it's the los ala most! It has the three-way strontium stretch?

AMY: I remember, north, south, and east by west. *That's* rather a handsome creation.

CHLOE [MODELLING HER RAGS]: It's dead-sea red. You can get it also in bone-slime lime and last-blast black.

AMY [GRANDLY]: The whole *creation* is rather a handsome creation! If only I could sit here forever, but the President's Ball is coming off, as indeed whose isn't—

LUELLA [MODELLING THE WEDDING GOWN]: Here's rather
a handsome creation—

(But AMY *falls upon* LUELLA's *rear with her teeth,
in a ravenous bite.*)

LUELLA: Aaaaaaaa!

(*She flees, dragging* AMY *a step before she gets
free;* AMY *on her knees roars like a lioness.*)

AMY: I'm so gluttonous I could eat a horse!
LUELLA [TO THE WITCHES]: Gluttony, see?
ALL: Gluttony, see?
AMY: Bring me my elephants, I want a whale to swal-
low, lock, stock, and bagel!

(TOM, DICK, *and* HARRY *at once come around the
rocks, bearing trays loaded with giant roasts, cham-
pagnes, fruits, bagels; they kneel with them to* AMY,
who seizes and gnaws on a leg. DINNY *approaches
the feast.*)

DINNY: Amy, I—don't know what to say—
AMY [SPITTING GRISTLE OUT]: Know where I live?
DINNY: No, I—
AMY [GRINNING]: I live on the wrong side of hell, you'll
have to come over sometime. Just a minute there,
B.O.!

(*She scrambles across the park to block* STONE-
HENGE's *exit with the baby carriage.*)

Bankers! Their middle name is avarice—
ZENOBIA, ULGA [AGHAST]: Avarice?
LUELLA: Avarice! Go away!

(*She pushes at* STONEHENGE.)

STONEHENGE [STIFFLY]: I am foreclosing on this.
AMY: On the carriage, natch, but what's inside is mine,
    I have the future of the world in there.
STONEHENGE: How much will you take for it in cash?
AMY: Twenty-five thousand.
STONEHENGE: Dollar forty-nine.
AMY: Ten thousand.
STONEHENGE: Dollar seventy-five.
AMY: Five thousand.
STONEHENGE: Dollar ninety-eight.
DINNY [WAILING]: Amy, that's our *baby!*
AMY: Sold. Goodbye, dear.

(STONEHENGE *slaps two bills in* AMY's *hands and
    endeavors to wheel the baby carriage off, but* LU-
    ELLA *hangs on to his coattails.*)

AMY [COUNTING]: Money money money money money—
DINNY: Amy, I'm warning you, you keep this up I'll ask
    for a divorce!
AMY [DARKLY]: Money is all I need. I have no treasure!
    Where's my baby? You forgot the baby?
DINNY: *I* forgot the baby!
AMY: But I can't get married without a baby! Every-
    one has a baby but me!
LUELLA: Envy, oi!
ALL: Envy, oi!

AMY: I envy you, I envy you, I envy you, I envy everyone in the world! Everyone's going to die of envy!

(*She darts for the* WITCHES' *pot, and comes up
with the black spray gun labelled with skull-and-
bones.*)

ZENOBIA: Stop her!
ULGA: She's got the atomic insecticide!
LUELLA: For people!

(AMY *makes for the other mortals.* DINNY *and the*
WITCHES *converge to grab her, but she knocks*
DINNY *staggering with a haymaker and breaks
through the* WITCHES. TOM, DICK, HARRY, DAWN,
CHLOE, *and* BUBBLES *separate, shrieking wildly, as*
AMY *charges them, this way, that way, up over the
rocks, around the tree and around the* WITCHES,
*under the park bench, spraying at now one, now
another; when the spray hits them, they petrify on
the spot, however they fall, but in lifelike postures.
In the midst of this bedlam* STONEHENGE *snatches
up the cleaver, and pursues* AMY; *she turns and
sprays him, and he sits petrified with the cleaver
upright in his hand; and* AMY *chases to finish off
the others.* DINNY *gets to his feet.* AMY *sees him
from afar, and comes on a beeline to him; she halts
with the spray gun aimed at his head.*)

AMY: You want to marry *me?*
DINNY [IN ANGUISH]: No!

(*And he waits. Then* AMY *hands him the spray
gun, meekly.*)

AMY: I'm not mad. Just terribly—terribly—

(*Her eyes close.*)

—slothful—

ALL [WHISPERING]: Slothful—

(AMY *sinks in center, puts her head on the floor, and goes to sleep. Now the music dies away, into silence, and the red sky pales to a sickly green. The* WITCHES *gather, to stare across at her.*)

DINNY: What the hell did you do to her? You put some kind of a spell on her!

ZENOBIA: But I had no idea it would work—

DINNY: It didn't work!

ZENOBIA: I mean I had no idea it wouldn't work. I mean—

LUELLA: It worked! She's got all those faults.

(*She points to* AMY *sleeping.*)

You see? Sloth! It came forth! All the faults you said come out—came out!

ZENOBIA: Well, it's simply a semantic mistake. I apologize.

ULGA [DARKLY]: Certainly is pretty inefficient, Zenobia.

ZENOBIA: I was not apologizing to you, Ulga.

LUELLA [TO ULGA]: I told her we couldn't change human nature.

ULGA: Yes, it was bad enough without making it worse. If she'd only listened to me—

ZENOBIA [IRRITABLY]: It was your idea, Ulga.

ULGA [ANGRILY]: My idea, but you ruined it the way you carried it out.

ZENOBIA: Well, accidents will happen, you know.

ULGA: No, I don't know! They don't happen to happen to me. I think maybe you're getting too old for your position, Zenobia.

ZENOBIA [THROUGH HER TEETH]: Don't get ambitious, Ulga!

ULGA: Well, when I do something it's efficient!

LUELLA: Yes, when Ulga does something it's efficient.

ZENOBIA: Exceedingly simple to be efficient when all it comes down to is chopping off people's heads! Some matters are more complex!

LUELLA: Yes, don't be so critical, Ulga, some matters are more complex. Nobody's perfect.

ULGA: Who isn't? *I* don't make mistakes like this!

ZENOBIA [ICILY]: If you're so perfect, why doesn't he marry you instead?

ULGA: Nobody's asked him!

LUELLA: Dinny, you want to marry Ulga instead?

DINNY [SAVAGELY]: Listen, will you tell me one thing, just *one* thing?

(*The witches look inquiringly.*)

How did you three get your jobs?

(*This is hardly a question, but they look at each other, trying to remember.*)

ZENOBIA: Well. In the Beginning—

DINNY: Drop dead! I've had enough of you wizard screwballs! I want to see a plain ordinary joe with American know-how—

LUELLA: Blow.

DINNY: —and second sight!

(*He lifts his horn, and blows tersely. They wait in silence. He blows a second time, tersely. Again they wait.* DINNY *then runs to the rocks, jumps on high, and blows a third time, loud and long, the first phrase of his song, in all directions. When he lowers the horn, it is* BEN *who reluctantly wends his way in.* JAKE *follows at a distance.*)

It's you, Ben?

BEN [A PAUSE]: Don't ask me to help you, Dinny.

DINNY: Ben, we got a little problem here—

BEN: Don't.

(DINNY *stares.*)

The answer's in the book.

DINNY: Nobody can open the damn book!

(BEN *holds out his key of the kingdom.*)

Don't give me that! I been through all that, I couldn't figure it out!

(BEN *after a moment drops the key on the book, and turns to leave.* DINNY *leaps after him, and spins him around.*)

That's your gratitude? I give you the eyes in your head, I give you a sight of apple trees and the stars and everything sweet in the world, you rat, you can't give *me* a minute?

BEN [FIERCELY]: Give me my blindness back!

(DINNY *strikes him across the face.* BEN *is staggered, and covers his eyes. When he lowers his hands, he is blind again, and he gropes;* DINNY *in fear avoids his hand.*)

BEN [THEN]: I give you five minutes. What do you want?

DINNY [WETTING HIS LIPS]: I want to make Amy—better.

BEN: Love her as she is.

DINNY: No.

BEN: What's wrong with her is what's wrong with the world, its seven unoriginal sins. I'd make peace with what is. Even her devils.

DINNY: No.

BEN [FINALLY]: Then rid her of them.

DINNY: *How?*

BEN: By the miracle of mortal breath, it turns even our death rattle into songs. I said mortal breath.

(DINNY's *hand comes out of his pocket, with the page; he weighs it.*)

We're all in death's hand, or who would listen to you?

DINNY: You mean—give up this page?

BEN: If you fail. Keep it if you make, and you will, a world that's— Ideal. It's only a breath away. I give you five minutes.

(*He begins to grope his way out, and his foot encounters* AMY; *he halts. In a low voice:*)

Forgive me.

JAKE: I'm here, Ben.

(*He comes to* BEN, *with his great key;* BEN *takes his arm and using his key as a cane, is led out by* JAKE. DINNY *stares after them. He looks from* AMY *to the* WITCHES *and back, making a decision, then wheels to them.*)

DINNY: How much time do I get?

ULGA: Five minutes.

DINNY: But I'm used to aeons!

ZENOBIA: Five minutes. Fail, and you give back the page!

(DINNY *considers it in his hand, a momentous choice.*)

DINNY: It's only a breath away.

(*Then he closes his fist on it, and nods.*)

I'll take my chances. Everybody's got to die some-time, I'll go along with the crowd.

ZENOBIA: Swear!

DINNY: I swear.

(ZENOBIA *and* ULGA *scurry back to their pot, summoning* LUELLA, *who stands in a twitch.*)

ZENOBIA: Very well, begin.

DINNY: Begin? What do you mean, begin? Where's her devils, what am I supposed to do?

ZENOBIA: Figure it out.
DINNY: Figure it out?!
ZENOBIA: Four and two-thirds minutes.

(LUELLA *runs to* DINNY, *frantically, to pull at him.*)

LUELLA: Dinny, you get out of here right away! It's a
    trap!
ZENOBIA [INDIGNANT]: Luella, this is low treason!

(ULGA *runs to grab* DINNY's *other arm, and tugs
him in the opposite direction.*)

DINNY: What kind of a trap?
LUELLA: Heads we win, heads you lose, that's what
    kind of a trap! That was a phony star we led you
    here with!
ULGA: I told you, Zenobia! She's caught it from him!
ZENOBIA: She'll catch it from me presently, and much
    worse!
LUELLA: I don't care, Zenobia! Dinny, you get out of
    here!
DINNY: I'm sunk. I'm sunk, if it's all a trap, how can I
    win against a witch who runs everything? *What
    have you got against me?*
LUELLA: You get out of here while you still have half
    of that page!

(*She lets go of* DINNY *to gesticulate, and* ULGA *collapses on her bottom.*)

DINNY: But Luella, I swore—
LUELLA: To who, *them?*

DINNY: I swore I'd make Amy—better. She's my girl,
    Luella!
LUELLA [TUGGING AGAIN]: Girls, I got a million of them,
    I'll give you all kinds every day, now you run, you
    run as far away as you can—
DINNY [BREAKS FREE]: Amy, should I run?

(AMY *is inanimate.* DINNY *cries out in desperation:*)

If it was a phony star I'm not supposed to be here!
LUELLA: Get out now, quick! Go on!

(*She drives at him,* DINNY *turns, and runs out.*
ZENOBIA *and* ULGA *converge on* LUELLA, *with throt-
tling hands ready;* LUELLA *retreats.*)

ZENOBIA [THROUGH HER TEETH]: Luella—
DINNY [OFFSTAGE]: Whee, look at that star shoot!

(*And he runs right back in; his finger pointing
follows the star around, down, and onto* AMY.)

That was no phony star.

(*He lets his hand fall, limply.*)

How much time is left?
ZENOBIA: Four minutes.

(*She and* ULGA *scurry back to the pot.* DINNY *speaks
to* AMY, *who is unmoving.*)

DINNY: I'm sorry I didn't know just now if I was com-
    ing or going. I'm only human, you know. I lost my
    head for a minute.

LUELLA: You're going to lose it forever in four minutes! You really made up your mind to stay?

DINNY: Yeah. Amy—

LUELLA: Then you're wasting good time. You still got four minutes!

ZENOBIA: Three and a half minutes.

DINNY: I'd like to spend them talking with Amy.

LUELLA: You better spend them figuring it out!

DINNY: Luella, I can't figure it out! I don't even know where to start looking for the goddam little devils. I haven't got a chance against the three of you, I give up.

LUELLA: Don't give up so easy! It's only two of them, I'm on your side.

ULGA: Luella, you'll pay for this!

LUELLA: You dry up, Ulga!

DINNY: So it's only two of them, look at them, I've seen more hope in coffins. I'm sunk.

ZENOBIA: Three minutes.

LUELLA: Where there's life, there's hope. Here I am!

DINNY: Yeah.

LUELLA: I'll give you ideas!

DINNY: Please.

LUELLA: Pick a lucky number.

DINNY: Luella, forget it.

LUELLA: Pick a lucky number!

DINNY [TO GET RID OF HER, WILDLY]: 1776!

LUELLA [THINKING]: Hm. Add them up.

DINNY: One, eight, fifteen, twenty-one.

LUELLA: Divide by three witches.

DINNY: Seven.

LUELLA: That's a lucky number!

DINNY [GETTING INTERESTED]: It is?

LUELLA: Sure, what comes in sevens around here?

(DINNY *begins to prowl around, hunting, and spots a mark on the ground.*)

DINNY: Pigeons?

LUELLA: Not pigeons!

DINNY: Shooting stars?

LUELLA: Not stars! What comes in sevens like mortal sins?

(DINNY *prowling spies* TOM, DICK, HARRY, STONE-HENGE, DAWN, CHLOE, *and* BUBBLES, *ranged more or less in a ring around* AMY, *frozen motionless.*)

DINNY [SLOWLY]: Mortal s—

LUELLA [STOPPING HIS MOUTH]: You're getting warm, go on!

DINNY: *Mortals?!*

LUELLA: Right!

DINNY [AMAZED]: They're the devils?

LUELLA: Sure.

DINNY: But they're human.

LUELLA: What's the difference?

DINNY: You mean if I can get them to leave her alone, she's pure?

LUELLA: Pure, sure!

DINNY: How can I get them to leave her alone?

ZENOBIA: Two and a half minutes.

DINNY [SHOUTS, WAVES HIS ARMS]: Leave her alone!

(*The mortals sit motionless.*)

It didn't work.

LUELLA: Try something else.

DINNY: I'll reason with them. Now look. Amy's the whole world to me, right? Right. I shouldn't have left her, but I left her, right? Wrong! But I got a chance to *put* it right, that star led me here, it's a second chance. That's a very rare thing. Now if you'll only leave her alone we can be happy, don't you want to see us happy? All right, then!

(*They sit motionless.*)

All wrong. They're not open to reason!

ZENOBIA: Two minutes.

LUELLA: Try something else.

DINNY: I'll buy them off. What do you want, money? I'll work for you, all my life, I'll work my fingers to the bone, I'll be your slave. You want cash down? Here, take my horn, it's solid gold, you can hock it for cash down.

(*He shouts at them.*)

What are you holding out for?

ZENOBIA: One and a half minutes.

LUELLA: You better try something else.

DINNY [NEAR TEARS]: I'll beg them. I'll get down on my knees to them. Please, please, won't you please leave her alone?

(*They sit motionless.*)

LUELLA: They're not doing it.

ZENOBIA: One minute.

DINNY [BROKEN]: I'm at the end of my rope. What can
    I do in the last minute? I'm through, I'm finished,
    I throw in the sponge.
LUELLA: Don't give up yet. Take the next breath.
DINNY: What for?
ZENOBIA: Half a minute.
LUELLA: Take the next breath!

(DINNY *takes a deep breath.*)

Now put it in the tuba!
DINNY: Where?
LUELLA: The witchemacallit!
DINNY: This?
LUELLA: Put it in!

(DINNY *lifts the horn to his mouth.*)

ZENOBIA [SHOUTING]: Fifteen seconds and the world is
    ours!

(*She and* ULGA *clap their hands over their ears.*
DINNY *plays the horn, and the lights dim to a fierce
spot on him and one on* AMY, *who shudders con-
vulsively. Presently* CHLOE *in silhouette moves,
takes a step to* AMY, *then backs off from her, towards* DINNY'S *horn.*)

CHLOE [VERY SLOW]:
        Sloth
        Came forth.
(*She turns, and goes off. One at a time, the others
repeat the same pattern, with* AMY *convulsive at*

*each voice. The lights commence to turn gradually
from red back to normal.)*

BUBBLES [SLOW]:

> *Envy
> Closed her eyes,
> And fled.*

TOM:

> *Gluttony
> Was fed.*

DICK:

> *Lust
> For an hour
> Slept.*

HARRY:

> *Anger
> Wept.*

DAWN:

> *Pride
> Her silks, her lace, herself abhorred,
> And hid her face.*

STONEHENGE:

> *And avarice
> Laid down his sword.*

(He puts the cleaver gently down at DINNY's *knees,
turns slowly, and goes off.* DINNY *has come to the
end of the tune. Nobody moves.)*

ZENOBIA [LOW]: The time is up.
LUELLA: Dinny. Open your eyes.

> *(*DINNY *lowers the horn, opens his eyes, and looks
> around.* ZENOBIA *puts her brow in her hand.)*

DINNY: They're gone.

(*He turns to* AMY, *who kneels alone.*)

Amy. They're all gone. Amy. Amy—

(*He begins to cry.*)

AMY: Dinny. I'm—

(*She stands, swaying.*)

I'm free, Dinny.
DINNY [EXALTED]: Amy. You remember me?
AMY [FARAWAY]: I remember you, Dinny.
DINNY: I did it. I did it.
LUELLA: But I helped.
DINNY: Luella helped.
LUELLA: I always say, take the next breath.

(ZENOBIA *lifts her face: she foresees it all.*)

ZENOBIA [LOW]: Where in the world did you learn to
      play like that?
DINNY: It was good, huh?
ZENOBIA: I thought it was—almost perfect.
AMY: Dinny.
DINNY: It's all perfect! I owe it all to this horn!

(*He leaps onto the bench. To the witches:*)

Listen, I'll play you a goodbye tune, anything you
want.
AMY [SCREAMING]: Dinny!

(*And she falls in a heap.* DINNY *is caught with the horn at his lips.*)

DINNY: Amy. Amy, what's the matter?

(*He jumps down, kneels beside her.*)

ZENOBIA: Dinny.

DINNY: Amy, say something to me. She must have fainted, she can't talk, but she's breathing all right—

ZENOBIA: She is not breathing.

DINNY: What? Amy!

(*He scrambles back from her in dread, then screams at* ZENOBIA.)

What have you done to her?

ZENOBIA: It is your doing. Was everything in the world not enough? You wished it all to be perfect as music: you have your wish.

DINNY: What are you telling me?

ZENOBIA: You mortals, you mortals are made of the earth and its excrement, which of you can live without it? Man and mud, out of its filth comes your strength, and humanity out of its devils. These were her natural and necessary ones. But you would love only something flawless: and what is flawless in the world is death.

DINNY: She's dead?

(*He comes over to her, whispers:*)

Amy. Don't be dead. She's only—a breath away. Amy, don't be dead.

(*He is crying, but he finds the horn in his hand, and shakes it savagely, as if to choke it.*)

Damn you, if I ever blow you again I hope to die!

(*He turns, and flings it away from him with all his might. Then he draws his wrist across his mouth, and turns back to* AMY. *He kneels to her.*)

LUELLA [TEARFULLY]: Dinny. I only tried to help you—

(DINNY *pauses, on one knee; when he answers* LU-ELLA *it is savage, through his teeth. She backs away from his venom.*)

DINNY: Don't talk to me. Get away from me, I don't want to see you again. What do you know, any of you? Mistakes, mistakes, everything I touch you turn inside out, is there one thing isn't a handful of blood and guts? *Stay away from me, you hear?* I don't want to see you again.

(*He cradles* AMY *in his arms. The witches are motionless, till* ULGA *takes a step toward* DINNY; ZENOBIA *lifts her finger, and* ULGA *freezes.*)

ZENOBIA [FINALLY]: The world is dead. Long live the world.

(*The curtain falls.*)

ACT III

IT IS ALMOST DAYBREAK IN THE PARK. A TINY GRAVEYARD NOW OCCUPIES THE SIDE OF THE HILLOCK, WITH A FEW TIPSY TOMBSTONES, AND AN OPEN GRAVE; THERE IS A CROOKED LITTLE FENCE AROUND IT.

BEN *in his rags is leaning against a tree, listening. He is alone.*

BEN [THOUGHTFULLY]: I think it's almost day. I can hear the crows, I get a lot of news from the crows. And the dew's here, on the grass and me, we've been out all night. What would it be like if the grass didn't drink the dew, and the grasshopper chew the grass, and the crow get the grasshopper? and a man never ate crow? Wouldn't be much of a world, it might as well never been wound up. But the way things are, you never can tell, the way things are: the world's in a tizzy, every minute it has a new twist. It's all to the good. Trouble, trouble's just the salt of the earth. I didn't make the world, but if I did, I think I'd make it the way it is. Remember, it's a blind man who says so.

(*He cocks his head.*)

I think they're coming.

(TOM, DICK, HARRY, *and* JAKE *come on, in their rags, carrying a coffin by its handles.*)

TOM: Let's put it down, it's killing me.

(*They put it down and sit on it, wiping their brows.*)

JAKE: I wouldn't have said she weighed so much. For all the world.

HARRY: You didn't, or I'd never have agreed to help out. Though I'd do anything for an old friend, but so much is too much.

JAKE: They say she had a bad heart, for all the world. It's the heart that's so heavy, you know.

TOM: I heard it was the head. She certainly had a bad head.

DICK: Yes, every minute a new twist.

HARRY: But then, she wasn't in it, most of the time.

TOM: Yes, that's true, too.

JAKE [A PAUSE]: They say she danced too much in the sun. For all the world she was light as a ball, on her feet.

HARRY: Well, she's certainly heavy on her—

DICK [COUGHS]: Please, old man. A little respect for the dead.

HARRY: Yes, yes, of course.

JAKE [A PAUSE]: They say she was a lovely sight, at her spinning, for all the world.

TOM: Yes, she was. I always wondered what she saw in him.

DICK: Did you?

TOM: Yes, didn't you?

DICK: No. I always wondered what he saw in her.

HARRY: Did you?

DICK: Yes, didn't you?

HARRY: No. I didn't see anything in either of them.
BEN: They say. They say they have eyes.

(DAWN, CHLOE, *and* BUBBLES *now are heard, chattering offstage to each other; the men's heads lift, to listen.*)

DAWN [FAST]: —then we had cocktails at the Astor then we had dinner at the Plaza then we went to this show then we had cocktails at the Plaza then we had dinner at the Astor then we went to the Copacabana—
CHLOE [OVERLAPPING]: —so I said to him you'd better take your hands off me I have a boy friend who used to be a wrestler he won't stand for anything funny honey I don't care if you are the head of the department—
BUBBLES [OVERLAPPING]: —but I didn't like the gray so I took the pink instead but the gray was very nice too so the next day I went back to exchange the pink for the gray but then I saw this *green* one—

(*They come on in a hustle from the opposite direction, in their rags, with black head veils.*)

JAKE: Turn it off!
BEN [WONDERING]: What's got into those crows?
JAKE: Can't you be serious with one foot in the grave?

(*The girls stop, and* CHLOE *delicately lifts her foot out of the grave.*)

CHLOE [WHISPERS]: Oh. I guess we're here.

(DINNY *comes wandering over the hill despondent,
tired and untidy, his jacket over his arm. His gaze
is caught by a passage of something overhead, we
hear it whiz; he pauses to stare at it.*)

JAKE: Hiya, Dinny.
DINNY [A PAUSE]: You see that?
JAKE: What?
DINNY [A PAUSE]: Nothing.

(*He comes to the group, looks down upon the coffin.*)

TOM: We got it this far, you see.
DINNY: I see.
DICK: Then the strangest thing happened, so we
    stopped.
DINNY: What?
DICK: Well, the further we carried it, the heavier it
    became.
HARRY: It seems unlikely, but do you think she's put-
    ting on weight?
DINNY [LOW]: Maybe your heart wasn't in it.
HARRY [TAKEN ABACK]: Why should *my* heart be *in* it?
TOM [WHISPERS]: He's thinking of himself again. Always
    himself.
JAKE: You okay, Dinny?
DINNY: I'm okay. I been thinking, though.
DICK: What about?
DINNY [TO THE COFFIN]: I been thinking, death is the
    last thing in life: but if you don't know about
    death, you don't know the first thing about life.
DICK: Ohhh?

DINNY: Well. I thank you for coming, I didn't want her to go without somebody—around, to remember. Let's take her in.

(*They lift the coffin and carry it to the enclosure. Before they can enter,* STONEHENGE, *in his rags, hurries on with upraised palm.*)

STONEHENGE: Just a moment, just a moment. Put it down, don't take another step. Now. What is it you want?

DINNY: Is this your cemetery?

STONEHENGE: I have a mortgage on it, yes.

DINNY: We want to bury a girl who—was the whole world.

STONEHENGE: Oh. Let me see, can I accommodate you? Yes, one vacancy. How much did you want to pay?

DINNY: Pay?

STONEHENGE: Pay.

DINNY: We just wanted to put her in the ground. Does that cost anything?

STONEHENGE: Yes, it costs a pretty penny. I have only one vacancy at five hundred.

DINNY: Five hundred what?

STONEHENGE: Dollars.

DINNY: Jeez. It costs more to die than to live.

STONEHENGE: True. But then it lasts longer.

DINNY: But I haven't got that kind of money.

STONEHENGE: Well, at times like this, snff, emotion always gets the better of me. What kind do you have?

DINNY: I've only got ninety-six bucks to my name.

STONEHENGE: Get out!

BUBBLES: I've got fifty.
BEN: I have twenty-three.
CHLOE: I'll put up thirty-two, honey.
JAKE: I'll give my last five.
STONEHENGE [CORDIALLY]: Come in.

(*They carry the coffin into the cemetery.*)

Don't put it in.

(*They set it down near the open grave.*)

I'll take that two hundred and six, if I may.

(*He passes around, collecting the money, and counts it.*)

Put it in.

(*They move the coffin in, and he covers it with a strip of store-window grass.*)

Now, I'll take care of everything, don't give it another thought. Shall we begin at once with the oration?
DINNY: If that's the right thing, sure.
STONEHENGE: Life's little ironies, we thought it would be a wedding, didn't we? A little closer, please.

(*They all gather around him, while he stands on the same elevation, takes from his pocket a clerical collar, and puts it on. They stand with bowed heads.*)

Dear friends. We are gathered here to witness the
last rites of this dearly departed image of earth.
What more need we say for all the world than that
she was God's noblest creation, who followed the
path of her maker, day and night? All of us loved
her: but only those who knew her well can say how
much we shall miss her pristine face, her sunny air,
her bountiful flesh. She was loving, modest, obeyed
the law—of gravitation—and was well balanced all
her days. She never said no to her children, or men.
She was dear to God, that is why he took her from
us. Amen.

(*A pause, then they stir.*)

CHLOE [SOFTLY]: That was beautiful.
DINNY: I'd like to add a few words.
STONEHENGE [OFFERING IT]: You want the collar?
DINNY. No.

(STONEHENGE *steps down,* DINNY *takes his place. He
gazes around at their faces, trying to find words,
then looks down at the grave.*)

No. Everything he said was a lie. She wasn't like
that at all. She was just a—thing made out of—
mud, like everyone else, she— She was no better
than any of us. Everything that's wrong in everyone
was wrong in her. No one loved her, enough. She
was no different from you and me, all I can say is,
there was—never another one like her. I could say
a lot more about her, but no matter what I'd say,
she—wasn't like any words at all. God bless you,
Amy.

STONEHENGE: Is that all?

(DINNY *doesn't move.*)

That's all.

(STONEHENGE *bows, and goes off. The others begin to turn away and drift out, murmuring among themselves.*)

BUBBLES [WHISPERING]: Beautiful service, wasn't it?
TOM: Yes, it was.
CHLOE: Only he shouldn't have said that at the end.
HARRY: No, I thought he spoiled the whole thing.
JAKE: Well, nothing's perfect.
DAWN: It was very nice but funerals are so sad I don't care for them at all—

(*And so on, till they are off.* BEN *is left alone, with* DINNY.)

BEN: Was everything he said a lie? Death opens our eyes. I mean, who wouldn't make a love song to the world, at its worst, the day it died?

(DINNY *stands unmoving. Then* BEN *turns, and blindly leaves.*)

DINNY [AFTER A MOMENT]: I wouldn't. I didn't. Amy, I'll make you a love song, now.

(*He whispers it at first, and only gradually works into it.*)

I turned my back, and a fog
Came round me,
I couldn't get back, and nightfall
Bound me
Away: now by day
I have come
To a house where she is dumb:

I talk to her now, and my love
Can't get in,
The doors are locked, and the windows
Let in
No light: and all night
She'll be here
With sweet nothing in her ear:

I come back, but the fog's
At my feet
And my echo's the one thing
I meet:

I turned my back, now my love
Is round me,
The house is dark, and the shutters
Hound me
With cries: while she lies
In the lee
Of a bed where I would be.

(*After a moment he drops to his knees.*)

Amy, what wouldn't I give—what wouldn't I give
—to go back to things as they were? I do. I do.

(*He puts his face in his hands, forward to the
earth, and lies still. Then the top of another grave
lifts up, and* ZENOBIA *and* ULGA *climb out;* ZENOBIA
*has the battered cuckoo clock. They stand, dusting
themselves off.* DINNY *rolls back.*)

What are you doing here?

ZENOBIA: Business.

ULGA: As usual.

DINNY: I don't want to do any more business with you.
I told you to stay away from me.

ZENOBIA: This is our last, our final-business meeting.
Where is Luella?

LUELLA: Here I am!

(*She comes flying down, with* DINNY's *horn in one
hand, the other holding an odd ring on her head.*
ULGA *and* ZENOBIA *regard it in astonishment.*)

ZENOBIA: In heaven's name, Luella!

ULGA: Looks ridiculous!

LUELLA: Only thing is, it gives me such a headache,
wow.

ULGA: Looks ridiculous!

ZENOBIA: Ulga! Telling me she was becoming part human, ha, and couldn't detect the truth when it
happened under your very nose!

ULGA: I wouldn't talk about noses if I was you, Zenobia.
If it happened under anybody's nose it was under—

DINNY [BITTERLY]: Go ahead, fight over a new hat. The
whole world can die and you—

LUELLA: It's not a hat! I earned it, I'm not a witch any
more, it's a halo.

DINNY: You made saint?

LUELLA: Angel!

ZENOBIA: How we shall ever cooperate now, I have no idea. Things will be worse. May we sit?

DINNY: Make yourselves to home. If you won't get out of here, I will.

(He starts out, they sit on the graves.)

ZENOBIA: Dinny, very few get out of here.

DINNY [WHEELING]: What are you, rubbing it in? You didn't do enough damage, you have to rub it in too? What are you doing with my horn?

LUELLA: I thought you'd want to take it with you.

DINNY: I said the next time I blow it I hope I die.

ULGA [GRINNING]: That's what she means.

DINNY: And the sooner the better.

ZENOBIA: It can be arranged. We came for that half page.

LUELLA [MOURNFULLY]: That's no way to talk, the sooner the—

DINNY: I know, take the next breath. Give me that horn.

(He snatches it, and blows one squawk.)

That's the next time.

(He looks up quickly, and follows with his eyes a passage overhead; we hear it whiz. The WITCHES look up.)

ZENOBIA: It's only a shooting star.

DINNY: Yeah. Lucky stars. This is where they led me, that's a pretty joke, hey? You think.

ZENOBIA: No. I don't. Now. With respect to the page. You promised—

DINNY: You promised me anything I wanted.

ZENOBIA: But you are insatiable! Never have we so put ourselves out to gratify a mortal's whims—

DINNY: Is this what I wanted?

ZENOBIA: Well! If the entire cosmos is to hang on a legalistic quibble like that—

DINNY: I didn't make the cosmos, I'm just passing through.

(*He takes the page from his pocket.*)

You need this pretty bad, huh?

ZENOBIA: The clock, Dinny. The clock is at a standstill, until that page goes back in the book.

DINNY: Okay. I'll make a deal. Give me two things, and you can have it.

ULGA [WARNING]: Zenobiaaaa—

ZENOBIA [WEARILY]: Name them.

DINNY: First. I want to stamp and stump and stomp on one of them stars till I kill it. With my own feet.

ZENOBIA: That can be arranged.

DINNY: Second. I want to read the book.

ZENOBIA [HAUGHTILY]: That cannot be arranged; it is much too priceless. Ulga, protect the book.

ULGA: What book?

ZENOBIA [STARING]: *The* book. Where—

ULGA: I haven't got the book. Luella.

LUELLA: Yes?

ULGA: You got the book?

LUELLA: What book?

ULGA: *The* book. Where did you—

LUELLA: Oh, *the* book. Zenobia, you had it last.

ZENOBIA [ANNOYED]: Had what?

LUELLA: The book.

ZENOBIA: What book, are you out of your—

LUELLA, ULGA: *The* book!

(*They stare at each other with widening eyes.*)

ZENOBIA: Good grief, girls, don't tell me we've lost it again!

(*They scatter, frantically searching behind rocks and tombstones, under store-window grass, and in the grave they came out of;* DINNY *clutches his head in disbelief.*)

DINNY: You can't have lost it! I got to read it, I got to know what it's all about! I did a lot of things and everything I did was wrong, I want to know why!

ZENOBIA [IN PASSING]: Such knowledge is beyond mortal reach.

(*She darts on,* DINNY *wheels after her.*)

DINNY: Don't give me that. I did everything, I had everything, and I didn't dig enough to fill in the eye of a needle. If I'm going to die one of these days I got a right to know why I was born, haven't I?

LUELLA [SEARCHING]: He's got a point there, Zenobia.

ZENOBIA [SEARCHING]: But the book contains all the secrets of the universe. It has never been scrutinized by mortal eye.

ULGA [SEARCHING]: Haven't even seen it ourselves, lately.

DINNY: Before I go out like a light I got to know what
it was for. You better find that book or I'm not
going out!

LUELLA [HEAD IN THE ASHCAN]: Here it is!

ZENOBIA: Glory be! Now, who could have put it in that
trash can?

(*They gather at the ashcan, while* LUELLA *gropes
head-first inside it.*)

LUELLA: It's stuck again.

(*She squirms.*)

I'm stuck, help!

(*She waves her legs in the air; and* ZENOBIA *and*
ULGA *each grab one, lift her out, and drop her.*)

ULGA: Turn it upside down.

(*They invert the ashcan, and bang on its bottom;
when they peer under it, only one of the great keys
slides out.* DINNY *comes to them.*)

DINNY [WITHERINGLY]: If you geniuses will let me?

(*He peers in, picks up the key.*)

Little thing we made up, called the lever?

(*He uses it as a pry-bar.* ZENOBIA *hastily extricating*

the book flees with it clutched to her bosom, ULGA
*after her; downstage, they endeavor once more to
open it, in vain.* LUELLA *meanwhile feels* DINNY'S
biceps, admiringly.)

LUELLA: Oh Dinny, how strong you are. You're a regu-
lar Simpson.
ZENOBIA: Stuck.
DINNY: I want to be strong in the head, that's where it
counts.

(*Turning*)

The book for the page! Is it a deal or not?
ULGA [BOUNTIFULLY]: Let him see it, Zenobia.
ZENOBIA [ASTONISHED]: Ulga, you know what is inscribed
on this flyleaf! "Knowledge is power." A mortal
who read this book would know as much as all the
deities and devils together.
DINNY: Just what I been looking for! The book for the
page, yes or no?
ULGA [MUTTERING]: It's stuck anyway. Let's *say* we'll
give it to him, then we'll get the half page, then
we'll give it to him! What can we—

(ZENOBIA *is staring at her, with pressed lips,* ULGA
falters.)

—lose?
ZENOBIA: Ulga, one virtue you do lack, richness of mind.
However, I'll outwit him.

(*To* DINNY)

Well, you drive a hard bargain, but we accept your terms. Give me the half page.

DINNY: No, you give me the book.

ZENOBIA: No, you must give me the page first.

DINNY: No, you give me the book first.

ZENOBIA: First the page!

DINNY: First the book!

ZENOBIA [A PAUSE]: It's a stalemate again.

DINNY: Somehow I don't *trust* you, Ulga. I'll give Luella the page with one hand, you give me the book in the other.

ULGA: No.

LUELLA: Why not?

ULGA: Somehow I don't *trust* you, Luella.

DINNY: It's a fair proposition.

ZENOBIA: But somehow I don't *trust* you, Dinny. Do you cross your heart?

DINNY: Cross my heart.

ZENOBIA: And hope to die?

DINNY [AND MEANS IT]: And hope to die.

ZENOBIA: Very well. Countdown! Ten, nine, eight, seven, six, five, four, three, two, one, *die*. I mean, do.

(DINNY *gives* LUELLA *the half page,* ULGA *puts the book in his hand. He almost collapses under its weight, clasps it in both arms.*)

DINNY: What makes it so heavy all of a sudden?

ZENOBIA: The wisdom of the ages, the mysteries of eternity.

DINNY: Sure is heavy.

(He staggers off with it to one side and sits with it; he examines its binding. LUELLA *drifts around him,* ZENOBIA *and* ULGA *watch him pityingly.)*

LUELLA: Poor Dinny.

ULGA: The fool. So easy to outwit.

ZENOBIA: The vanity of human aspirations, one would think he might have learned by now, but what can one expect from these mortal puppets—

DINNY: What is this keyhole?

ZENOBIA [CONTEMPTUOUS]: What keyhole?

DINNY: This keyhole.

(He inserts the great key in the binding, and the book springs open. DINNY *is elated.)*

I figured it out!

ZENOBIA: Egad!

ULGA: He figured it out!

DINNY: *I figured it out!*

LUELLA: He figured it out!

(She runs to him, excitedly.)

You have to turn to the page marked Secrets of the Universe. It's under C.

DINNY: I got it!

(He begins to read it raptly. ZENOBIA *darts to* LU-ELLA.*)*

ZENOBIA: I'll take that page now. Hurry!

LUELLA [RETREATING]: Somehow I don't *trust* you, Zenobia, you're not on the up and up.

DINNY [READING, ASTOUNDED]: Wow!

(*They freeze.*)

ZENOBIA: He has the book, does he not, he even has it
  open! Quick, before it's too late!
LUELLA: Well, he has to have some time to read it.
ZENOBIA [DESPERATE]: He can't read it, it will take him
  forever!
DINNY [READING, ASTOUNDED]: Hey, hey, hey, hey!

(*They freeze.*)

LUELLA: Dinny, you haven't got forever—
DINNY: Listen to this, will you? "Every cloud has a silver
  lining!" *Boy!*

(*He wets a finger, whips a page over.*)

ULGA [DESPERATE]: Give it to her, Luella!
LUELLA: Just hold your horses. Plenty of time, we could
  let him have a few minutes.
ZENOBIA: But he's learning all our secrets!
DINNY [ECSTATIC]: "The best things in life are *free!*"
  Omigod!

(*He whips a page over.*)

ZENOBIA [ANGRILY]: Give me that page, Luella, or I'll—
  I'll—
LUELLA: What, what? I'm not under you any more,
  Zenobia, you can't scare me.
DINNY: "You can't have everything!"

(*He whips a page over.*)

"Everything comes to him who waits!"

ZENOBIA [TO LUELLA]: You ingrate! You parvenu!

LUELLA: Sticks and stones can break my bones, you know what I could do if I want? I could give him a third chance.

ULGA: A third chance!

ZENOBIA: I never heard of such a thing!

LUELLA: You better be nice to me or I'll give him a third chance.

DINNY: "Where there's a *will* there's a *way!*"

ULGA: [SCREAMING]: I told you I didn't trust her! Zenobia, you should listen to me sometimes.

ZENOBIA [SCREAMING]: I did listen to you! You said what can we lose?

ULGA: Well, you said you'd outwit him!

ZENOBIA: How could I know she'd betray us again? We've been nursing a snake in our bosom!

LUELLA: A what?

ZENOBIA: A snake!

LUELLA: Dinny, how would you like a third chance?

DINNY: "Try, try again!"

ZENOBIA [FALLING ON HER KNEES]: Luella, I beseech you, I implore you—

LUELLA: That's better.

ULGA [FALLING TO HER KNEES]: Don't do this to us, Luella.

ZENOBIA: It's not only us: it's the entire world. Your infatuation with this boy is leading you into a great injustice.

LUELLA: How come?

DINNY: "It is later than you think!" ???

ZENOBIA: What of your other responsibilities? The world is waiting for you. What of Maggie Callahan's baby?

LUELLA: Oh. Poor baby. I forgot.

ULGA: What about Oscar Dibble's mother-in-law in the bathroom?

LUELLA: Yes. Poor Oscar.

DINNY: "It's *never* too late!"

LUELLA [SADLY]: You're right. Dinny, it's too late.

DINNY [SOFTLY]: "Love makes the world go round." Yes. Oh, yes.

(*He closes* HIS *eyes, takes a breath, and looks up, slowly.*)

You know that's the whole nut in a shell? This is the best book I ever read.

LUELLA: Dinny, I can't give you a third chance.

DINNY: But I didn't ask for one. You couldn't bring Amy back out of the grave, could you?

ULGA: Naturally not.

LUELLA: Not naturally.

DINNY: Well, then, what's the good of it? I was all that time looking, I thought if I saw it I'd know it, and I saw it and I didn't know it. Till now. I wanted something no one else had: and it was Amy. Love makes the world go round, but I don't want to go round now without Amy.

(*He holds the book out to* ULGA, *who comes, takes it from him.*)

Whenever my time is up. One thing you can be sure of.

LUELLA: Which?

DINNY: The rest of my life I'm gonna put it to use. Everything I learned from that book.

LUELLA [GRIEVING]: Dinny.

DINNY: No, I'm not gonna waste a minute! I learned my lesson, once and for all. You can't have everything, even a little is gravy while you got it. No more chasing after—

(*He gazes overhead; we hear the star whiz.*)

Hey, wait a minute. Those stars.

ZENOBIA: Yes?

DINNY: I got to get one of those stars.

ULGA: What does that matter now? Zenobia, we've—

DINNY [QUICKLY]: You said I could.

ZENOBIA: Yes, I said he could.

DINNY: Look, one's landing right over there, see? It'll only take me a minute.

LUELLA: I'll wait.

DINNY: Just give me a minute.

(*He runs off, chasing it with his finger aloft.*)

LUELLA: I'll give him more than a minute. Ten minutes.

ULGA [AT THE BREAKING POINT]: Zenobia, we've wasted so much time on this case already—

LUELLA: But whatever he's learned, he deserves a chance to apply it. For ten minutes.

ULGA [SHOUTING]: I can't wait ten minutes more, I'll have a nervous breakdown!

LUELLA: If he could just apply it for ten minutes, even, he won't be altogether a failure.

ZENOBIA: I can see that. And I'm rather fond of him

myself. I think we can spare him ten minutes out of eternity.

LUELLA: Good, so we'll give him a little chance. Now let's clear this graveyard away.

ULGA: Why? It's handy!

LUELLA: Because he has to start with a clean slate, that's why. Can't have him stuck with all these mistakes. We'll put him right back where we found him, before the clock stopped. Now help me.

(*She begins to run around, clearing the graveyard, and* ZENOBIA *and* ULGA *help her, gathering the tombstones, fence, store-window grass, while they mutter their chant, slowly, not necessarily in unison.*)

ZENOBIA, LUELLA, ULGA:

> *Last chance. For Dinny.*
> *With a fat and a butt and a fat butt skinny*
> *Last chance. For Dinny.*
> *World's in a tizzy,*
> *Chockful of kukes,*
> *Can't have it stuck*
> *With all their mistukes,*
> *Time never stops,*
> *It's always in flukes,*
> *So back. With Dinny.*
> *For a fat and a butt and a fat butt skinny*
> *And a one,*
> *More,*
> *Small,*
> *Last,*
> *Chance.*

(And they are off with everything, including the horn, leaving the park just as it was in the very beginning.)

DINNY [OFFSTAGE]: Whee, look at that star shoot!

(He comes running back on, his eyes aloft, pointing, and the whizzing star leads him straight to The Fission Hole door, which opens; and AMY shakes a tableclothful of pretzels into his face.)

Hey!

AMY: Oh, excuse me, Dinny. I didn't know you were still here.

DINNY: Sure I'm still here, where do you think I'm in the, clouds? What's your name, again?

AMY: Amy.

DINNY: Oh. Hiya.

AMY: You want to wait and walk me home?

DINNY: Nah, if I walk you home the first thing I know I'll be married.

AMY: Of all the conceit!

(She goes in again, shutting the door. DINNY shouts after her.)

DINNY: Well, I got other things to do in the world! I gotta—

(LUELLA scurries in, brandishing the horn.)

LUELLA: Dinny, you dope!

DINNY: What?

(*He turns, sees her, is horrified.* LUELLA *bangs him over the head with the horn; he staggers and falls, unconscious.*)

LUELLA [OVER HIM]: Won't you ever learn? Can't you get *anything* through that skull? It wasn't in the book *she* should die, the clock is stopped, so it didn't happen! I brought her back, it's your last chance at this world, you going to be a dumbbell forever? Now I'll give you a *fourth chance.*

(*She drops the horn, and shrieks:*)

Help, murder, police!

(*She scurries behind a tree, hiding.* AMY *comes running out of The Fission Hole, spies* DINNY, *and runs to him, kneels, lifts him up. He opens his eyes.*)

AMY: Are you all right?
DINNY [BEWILDERED]: What are you, a quick-change artist?
AMY: Did you faint?
DINNY: Why did you hit me over the head for?
AMY: Why did I—

(*She stands, letting him flop.*)

You're impossible!
DINNY: No, no, just—

(*He gets to his knees.*)

—hard to believe. I got it wrong, it couldn't have been you, this was the ugliest female I ever laid eyes on.

(LUELLA *behind the tree starts crying.* DINNY *cocks his head.*)

Did you hear something?

AMY: What?

DINNY: I thought I heard that tree crying.

AMY: Look, are you well? I mean, in the head?

DINNY: I don't know, I never heard a tree crying before. What's your name?

AMY [WRATHFULLY]: My name is Amy!

DINNY: That's what I thought it was. Mine's Dinny.

AMY: That's what *I* thought it was, so we have a lot in common!

DINNY: You know, you're very pretty.

AMY: I think you'd better get up off your knees. Unless you expect to propose.

DINNY [SCRAMBLING UP]: Propose! All I said was you're pretty.

AMY: You said very pretty.

DINNY: All right, very pretty, that's a long way from getting married. I got other things to do in the world. I gotta chase a star now and then, for instance, I was just chasing one when I ran into you.

AMY: What for?

DINNY: Because I thought it might lead me to what I'm after.

AMY: Did it?

DINNY: Nah, it got away. Temporarily.

AMY: Are you still chasing it?

DINNY: Of course I'm still chasing it, what does it look like I'm doing?

AMY: It looked like you were talking to me.

DINNY: I don't know where you women get these ideas! What do you suppose is *ailing* that tree?

AMY: I think you'd better walk me home.

DINNY: What for?

AMY: Breakfast. I think what you need is a good strong cup of—

LUELLA [IN TEARS]: Love. Love.

DINNY: Wait a minute. Something's wrong with my head.

AMY: Yes, I think so.

DINNY: I mean, I can't hear what I'm thinking. Something's going on in there, I wish I could make it out. Some saying. Love. Love is—

(Jubilantly, but ending in some doubt)

I learned my lesson, once and for all, love is free, the best things in life make the world go round?

AMY: I never heard that saying before.

DINNY [DUBIOUSLY]: It's an old saying.

LUELLA [WEEPING]: And every time is a second chance.

DINNY: And every—every—

LUELLA: —time is a second chance.

DINNY: No, I can't make it out.

AMY: You want to walk me home or not? I make perfect coffee!

(DINNY regards her in an agony of indecision, backs away from her, rounds on his heel scanning the sky

for stars, gazes back at AMY *from a distance, and
makes up his mind. He cups his hands to his
mouth, and hollers in all directions.*)

DINNY: Hey! Hey, everybody! Everybody in this park,
comes here, I got a speech to make!
AMY [CALLING]: Everybody! Everybody!

(*And everybody from the play, no longer in rags
but as we first saw each, comes running in, as*
DINNY *leaps onto the rock to address them.*)

DINNY: I got a thing to tell you. She says she makes
perfect coffee.
ALL: Perfect coffee?!
DINNY: If it's perfect, I'll take a chance! I want to say
to you—*I'm gonna walk her home!*

(*They cheer him.*)

Now. Where'd I put that horn?

(*He finds it, picks it up.*)

AMY: It looks dented. Can you still play it?
DINNY: Can I still play it! Oh Amy, Amy, this is how I
live and breathe and talk. Now you listen to me—

(*But in the act of lifting it to his mouth he pauses,
troubled, and gazes upon it. Then*)

I mean. I know it's not everything in life, Amy, a
little wind, but—Amy, what can I do? When I'm

down I want to blow the horn, when I'm up I
want to blow the horn, what can I do?

AMY [A PAUSE]: Blow the horn.

ALL [PLEASED]: Blow the horn!

(DINNY *lifts it, and plays the same song.* AMY *looks
up, follows with her eyes a passage of something,
we hear it whiz, then she looks quickly at* DINNY,
*whose eyes are closed; she glances up again, then
takes him by the arm, and with* DINNY *still playing,
they walk off together. The crowd snake-dances
after them, singing:*

> *Don't know why I came here,*
> *Just followed my nose:*
> *Couldn't say what I'm after,*
> *Can't wait till it shows:*
> *Can't give you its name here,*
> *Heard it lies in my way—*

Until they are all gone, leaving LUELLA *onstage
alone. The horn continues offstage until further
notice.* LUELLA *sobs.*)

LUELLA: Goodbye, Dinny.

(ZENOBIA *and* ULGA *come on, with the book and
cleaver. They stare at* LUELLA.)

ZENOBIA: What on earth's the matter, child?

LUELLA [WHIMPERING]: Everything. I feel just terrible.
I love him so, and he said I was the—said I was—
the ugliest—

ULGA: Well, aren't you?

ZENOBIA: Ten minutes are past. Did he make good?

LUELLA: Yes. He made good.

ZENOBIA: Then his time is up.

LUELLA: I know. Here's the page.

> (*She holds it out sideways, not looking, and* ULGA *snatches it.*)

ZENOBIA: Don't cry. Come, work will make you feel better.

> (*She sits at the caldron.*)

Ulga, pull the night back over us.

> (ULGA *runs across the park with her fists upraised, and night covers the sky.*)

Put the page back in the book. Come, Luella.

> (LUELLA *sits most reluctantly,* ULGA *squats with the book and page, and* ZENOBIA *hovers her hands over the caldron.*)

Ready?

ULGA: Yes.

ZENOBIA, LUELLA, ULGA [VERY SLOW]:
>
> *This is how the world will end,*
> *In a stew, in a stew,*
> *Kiss me, foe, and weep me, friend,*
> *Parting's old, parting's new:*
> *Ashes to ashes, though all the tongues bawl,*

Dust unto dust, over great, over small,
Atom to atom, and let the sun fall:
Spill the brew.

(ZENOBIA *spills it, and* ULGA *strikes a great blow*
with the cleaver. Instantly, far off, the sound of
DINNY'S *horn stops. The three* WITCHES *lift their*
heads, listening to the silence. A pause.)

LUELLA [FAINTLY]: Goodbye, Dinny.
ULGA [LOW]: Goodbye, Dinny.
ZENOBIA [SLOWLY]: Goodbye, Dinny.

(*A pause*)

I'll miss hearing him play.
LUELLA [CRYING]: Who ever started dying anyway?
  Ulga, I *hate* you!
ULGA: I didn't start it.
ZENOBIA: No. She does only what must be done.
LUELLA: Why must it?
ZENOBIA: I don't know. This is how the world was—
  made—

(*She catches her breath, and averts her face.*)

ULGA: It's happened millions of times. What are both
  of you—crying about—

(*She too chokes up, and they sit weeping, three*
mourners.

After a moment there is a startling burst of DINNY'S

trumpet from one side, and of hot music from The
Fission Hole opposite. AMY *and* DINNY *come back*
through the park, swinging along in a great hurry.)

DINNY: Sure got dark awful quick. Listen, they started
without me.
AMY: The day just flew by. I don't understand it.
DINNY: Must be the shortest day of the year.

(They go into The Fission Hole; the music fades
down. The WITCHES *have lifted their grieving heads*
in unison to stare after them, utterly astounded.
Slowly and dazedly they look at each other.)

ZENOBIA [SHAKILY]: That's a—very—unusual young
man—
LUELLA: That *never* happened before—
ULGA: Did you forget to spill it?

(She inverts the caldron again.)

ZENOBIA: These mortals must be—getting stronger—
I—

*(*ULGA *suddenly grabs the halves of the page and*
peers at them.)

ULGA [HOARSELY]: No.
ZENOBIA: No what?
ULGA: We made a little mistake here.
LUELLA: We did?
ULGA: I don't think it's his name on this page.
LUELLA [JOYOUSLY]: It isn't?

ULGA: It's *almost* his, but—

ZENOBIA: Whose is it?

ULGA [IN AGONY]: Minnie Jones.

ZENOBIA: *Minnie* Jones! Ulga, this is the last straw!

ULGA: I'm sorry, Zenobia.

ZENOBIA [FURIOUSLY]: Apologies are useless! I've never liked you, I always thought you a particularly repulsive and inhumane person—

LUELLA: Zenobia, don't be unkind—

ULGA: No, I have my faults—

ZENOBIA: —but I put up with them for the sake of your efficiency. Now if you intend to bungle matters in this way—

ULGA: I didn't intend to—

LUELLA: She didn't intend to—

ZENOBIA: —then I don't see what I can do but ask to have you replaced by somebody who—

ULGA: It won't happen again, Zenobia. It's my eyes, they're going back on me.

LUELLA: She won't do it again, Zenobia.

ZENOBIA: How can she be sure?

LUELLA: She can get glasses!

ULGA: I'll get glasses!

ZENOBIA: Well, see that you do! And immediately, before you take another name. The time and trouble you've caused us! Put the sun back, Luella.

(LUELLA *dances across the park with hands upraised, and the daylight comes back.* ZENOBIA *shakes herself.*)

My, that feels better.

LUELLA: I'll say! We're lucky.

ULGA: He's lucky too.

ZENOBIA: Well, *that* remains to be seen. Though I wish him luck.

(DINNY *and* AMY *come out of the night club, blinking at the sunlight.*)

DINNY: Sure is changeable weather.

AMY: I've never seen anything like it. The night just flew by.

DINNY: Must be time to walk you home again.

AMY: Time just seems to fly by.

DINNY [STOPS]: Hey.

AMY: Yes?

DINNY: I wonder—

AMY: What, Dinny?

DINNY: I wonder if it could be love?

AMY: I wonder.

(*They stare at each other.*)

DINNY: Listen, I think it could be love.

(*He takes her hand and they start through the park, gazing at each other. So they bump into* LU-ELLA. DINNY *looks upon her blissfully.*)

Hello.

LUELLA: Hello.

(DINNY *and* AMY *pass on.*)

DINNY: Wasn't she a nice-looking lady?

(They go out. LUELLA is staggered, in a rapture.)

LUELLA: Did you hear what he said about me?

ZENOBIA: I heard.

LUELLA: Did you hear what he said, Ulga?

ULGA: Certainly.

LUELLA: He said I was a nice-looking lady. Oh, I wish
   him luck!

ZENOBIA: So do I.

ULGA: So do I.

LUELLA: Then let's wish him luck!

*(The three of them link arms and do a little jig,
chanting.)*

ZENOBIA, LUELLA, ULGA:

> *All hail, to Dinny!*
> *With a good and a bye and*
> *   a good bye minnie*
> *And a hail, to Dinny!*
> *He followed his star,*
> *What more can we say,*
> *He never could find it*
> *By night or by day,*
> *Cause every damn time*
> *Love*
> *It got in his way,*
> *So hail, to Dinny!*
> *With a good and a luck and*
> *   a good luck dinny*
> *And a hail,*
> *Hail,*
> *Hail,*
> *Hail—*

(It begins to hail, and they cover their heads and run about looking for shelter. They find it under a tree, where they all huddle, shivering, peering forth, three woebegone and wretched creatures, muttering to themselves.

This seems to be the end of the play.

When the curtain rises for the calls, the stage is empty. DAWN, CHLOE, *and* BUBBLES *come dancing in, freeze with their heads together, and sing:)*

DAWN, CHLOE, BUBBLES:
> I'm a girl that likes to go along,
> Give me lovin', tell me so along,
> Give me gaga, googoo, gumgum, don't
>   forget to bring your dough along:
> Three fun-lovers are we,
> Are we.

(They bow and dance off opposite. STONEHENGE *comes in, making notes in a ledger; he gazes around, scratching his head.)*

STONEHENGE: Peculiar. I could have sworn I left a grave-yard here.

(BEN and JAKE come in opposite.)

JAKE: This is a new kind of operation, Ben, it'll fix up your eyes.
BEN: What do they do?
JAKE: They take out your heart and make new eyeballs out of it.

BEN: Isn't that bad on the heart?

JAKE: They got a new operation for that, they take out your brain and put it where your heart should be.

BEN: Sounds pretty modern.

STONEHENGE: Either of you men see a graveyard strolling around here?

JAKE: No.

BEN: But then what do they use for a brain?

JAKE: They got a new operation for that, they're doing away with it altogether.

BEN: What's it called?

JAKE [HAT TO BREAST]: Loyalty.

BEN: I get my blindness back?

(*They bow, and go off.* STONEHENGE *gazes around, regretfully.*)

STONEHENGE: And I expected to be doing such a brisk trade. Well, it's financial or intellectual, my bankruptcy or yours. Any bets?

(*He bows and goes off.* TOM, DICK, *and* HARRY *come running in from opposite directions, pass each other, scurry back, and line up at attention.*)

TOM, DICK, HARRY:

We are the kings of the world, of the world,
We pass all the laws, we get no applause,
Everything we say is purely applesaws:
But we are the kings of the kingdom without
Where the kings will get you if you don't
    watch out!

(They bow and dance off. DINNY comes on, horn in hand, and takes a solo bow. Then AMY comes on, pushing the baby carriage, and bows. They join over the baby carriage.)

DINNY: What do you want him to be when he grows up, Amy, a doctor?
AMY: A lawyer.
DINNY: Nah, a doctor.
AMY: No, a lawyer.
DINNY: I said, a doctor!
AMY: And I said, a lawyer!

(The BABY sits up in the carriage, pointing over-head; we hear a star whiz.)

BABY: Whee, look at that star shoot!

(DINNY and AMY gawk, look at each other, make a helpless gesture, and sing to the BABY.)

DINNY, AMY:

> *Didn't hear what you looked like,*
> *Only heard I was due:*
> *Didn't know what I'm here for,*
> *Guess it was you.*

(During which they push the baby carriage off together, as ZENOBIA, LUELLA, and ULGA in heavy spectacles come crouch-running on, bowing and peering after them; ULGA has the book, ZENOBIA the clock.)

LUELLA: Good luck! What's their fortune in the book?

ULGA [CONSULTING IT]: They lived happily ever after. It says here.

ZENOBIA: Now we must take that Minnie Jones. Decapitation, if I recall.

ULGA: That's right, Zenobia.

ZENOBIA [NEGLIGENTLY]: Look in the book, see where she is.

ULGA: Right now?

ZENOBIA: Yes, right now.

(ULGA *flips a page, runs a finger down.*)

ULGA: Right now she's at the Blahdeblah Theatre.

ZENOBIA [FROWNING]: But that's where we are.

ULGA: First row on the aisle.

LUELLA: That must be her there.

ULGA: That's her.

ZENOBIA: Seize her!

(*The three of them fly over the footlights. Poor* MINNIE *rises to flee, shrieking, but they seize her, and* LUELLA *and* ULGA *bear her off, screaming for help, up the aisle.* ZENOBIA *looks sharply around at the audience; her voice rings out.*)

You mortals, what are you snickering at? The clock has been stopped long enough: go home! It has begun to tick again. Listen.

(*She holds the clock aloft, and indeed it is ticking clearly and slowly, like a metronome. The cuckoo pops out, and chirps cuckoo.*)

Each tick is one heartbeat the less in each of you.
Make the most of it, go home, be about your—

(*Her voice becomes pleasantly devastating*)

—nuclear business. Savor the world, while you
have it. Now get out, get out, get out!

(*She runs up the aisle after* LUELLA *and* ULGA. *And
this is really the end of the play.*)

THE
MIRACLE
WORKER

———

A PLAY IN THREE ACTS

"At another time she asked, 'What is a soul?'
'No one knows,' I replied; 'but we know it is
not the body, and it is that part of us which
thinks and loves and hopes.' . . . [and] is in-
visible. . . . 'But if I write what my soul
thinks,' she said, 'then it will be visible, and
the words will be its body.' "
                          —ANNIE SULLIVAN, 1891

THE PLAYING SPACE *is divided into two areas by a more or less diagonal line, which runs from downstage right to upstage left.*

THE AREA *behind this diagonal is on platforms and represents the Keller house; inside we see, down right, a family room, and up center, elevated, a bedroom. On stage level near center, outside a porch, there is a water pump.*

THE OTHER AREA, *in front of the diagonal, is neutral ground; it accommodates various places as designated at various times—the yard before the Keller home, the Perkins Institution for the Blind, the garden house, and so forth.*

THE CONVENTION OF THE STAGING *is one of cutting through time and place, and its essential qualities are fluidity and spatial counterpoint. To this end, the less set there is, the better; in a literal set, the fluidity will seem merely episodic. The stage therefore should be free, airy, unencumbered by walls. Apart from certain practical items—such as the pump, a window to climb out of, doors to be locked—locales should be only skeletal suggestions, and the movement from one to another should be accomplishable by little more than lights.*

CHARACTERS

A DOCTOR

KATE

KELLER

HELEN

MARTHA

PERCY   *Negros children*

AUNT EV

JAMES

ANAGNOS

ANNIE SULLIVAN

VINEY

BLIND GIRLS

A SERVANT

OFFSTAGE VOICES

TIME: *The 1880's.*

PLACE: *In and around the Keller homestead in Tuscumbia, Alabama; also, briefly, the Perkins Institution for the Blind, in Boston.*

ACT I

Inside, three adults in the bedroom are grouped around a crib, in lamplight. They have been through a long vigil, and it shows in their tired bearing and disarranged clothing. One is a young gentlewoman with a sweet girlish face, KATE KELLER; *the second is an elderly* DOCTOR, *stethoscope at neck, thermometer in fingers; the third is a hearty gentleman in his forties with chin whiskers,* CAPTAIN ARTHUR KELLER.

DOCTOR: She'll live.

KATE: Thank God.

(*The* DOCTOR *leaves them together over the crib, packs his bag.*)

DOCTOR: You're a pair of lucky parents. I can tell you now, I thought she wouldn't.

KELLER: Nonsense, the child's a Keller, she has the constitution of a goat. She'll outlive us all.

DOCTOR [AMIABLY]: Yes, especially if some of you Kellers don't get a night's sleep. I mean you, Mrs. Keller.

KELLER: You hear, Katie?

KATE: I hear.

KELLER [INDULGENT]: I've brought up two of them, but this is my wife's first, she isn't battle-scarred yet.

KATE: Doctor, don't be merely considerate, will my girl be all right?

DOCTOR: Oh, by morning she'll be knocking down Captain Keller's fences again.

KATE: And isn't there anything we should do?

KELLER [JOVIAL]: Put up stronger fencing, ha?

DOCTOR: Just let her get well, she knows how to do it better than we do.

(*He is packed, ready to leave.*)

Main thing is the fever's gone, these things come and go in infants, never know why. Call it acute congestion of the stomach and brain.

KELLER: I'll see you to your buggy, Doctor.

DOCTOR: I've never seen a baby, more vitality, that's the truth.

(*He beams a good night at the baby and* KATE, *and* KELLER *leads him downstairs with a lamp. They go down the porch steps, and across the yard, where the* DOCTOR *goes off left;* KELLER *stands with the lamp aloft.* KATE *meanwhile is bent lovingly over the crib, which emits a bleat; her finger is playful with the baby's face.*)

KATE: Hush. Don't you cry now, you've been trouble enough. Call it acute congestion, indeed, I don't see what's so cute about a congestion, just because it's yours? We'll have your father run an editorial in his paper, the wonders of modern medicine, they don't know what they're curing even when they cure it. Men, men and their battle scars, we women will have to—

(*But she breaks off, puzzled, moves her finger before the baby's eyes.*)

Will have to—Helen?

(*Now she moves her hand, quickly.*)

Helen.

(*She snaps her fingers at the baby's eyes twice, and her hand falters; after a moment she calls out, loudly.*)

Captain. Captain, will you come—

(*But she stares at the baby, and her next call is directly at her ears.*)

Captain!

(*And now, still staring,* KATE *screams.* KELLER *in the yard hears it, and runs with the lamp back to the house.* KATE *screams again, her look intent on the baby and terrible.* KELLER *hurries in and up.*)

KELLER: Katie? What's wrong?
KATE: Look.

(*She makes a pass with her hand in the crib, at the baby's eyes.*)

KELLER: What, Katie? She's well, she needs only time to—

KATE: She can't see. Look at her eyes.

(*She takes the lamp from him, moves it before the child's face.*)

She can't *see!*
KELLER [HOARSELY]: Helen.
KATE: Or hear. When I screamed she didn't blink. Not an eyelash—
KELLER: Helen. Helen!
KATE: She can't *hear* you!
KELLER: *Helen!*

(*His face has something like fury in it, crying the child's name;* KATE *almost fainting presses her knuckles to her mouth, to stop her own cry.*

The room dims out quickly.

Time, in the form of a slow tune of distant belfry chimes which approaches in a crescendo and then fades, passes; the light comes up again on a day five years later, on three kneeling children and an old dog outside around the pump.

The dog is a setter named BELLE, *and she is sleeping. Two of the children are Negroes,* MARTHA *and* PERCY. *The third child is* HELEN, *six and a half years old, quite unkempt, in body a vivacious little person with a fine head, attractive, but noticeably blind, one eye larger and protruding; her gestures are abrupt, insistent, lacking in human restraint, and her face never smiles. She is flanked by the*

*other two, in a litter of paper-doll cutouts, and
while they speak* HELEN's *hands thrust at their
faces in turn, feeling baffledly at the movements
of their lips.*)

MARTHA [SNIPPING]: First I'm gonna cut off this doctor's legs, one, two, now then—
PERCY: Why you cuttin' off that doctor's legs?
MARTHA: I'm gonna give him a operation. Now I'm
   gonna cut off his arms, one, two. Now I'm gonna
   fix up—

(*She pushes* HELEN's *hand away from her mouth.*)

You stop that.
PERCY: Cut off his stomach, that's a good operation.
MARTHA: No, I'm gonna cut off his head first, he got
   a bad cold.
PERCY: Ain't gonna be much of that doctor left to fix
   up, time you finish all them opera—

(*But* HELEN *is poking her fingers inside his mouth,
to feel his tongue; he bites at them, annoyed, and
she jerks them away.* HELEN *now fingers her own
lips, moving them in imitation, but soundlessly.*)

MARTHA: What you do, bite her hand?
PERCY: That's how I do, she keep pokin' her fingers
   in my mouth, I just bite 'em off.
MARTHA: What she tryin' do now?
PERCY: She tryin' *talk*. She gonna get mad. Looka her
   tryin' talk.

(HELEN *is scowling, the lips under her fingertips
moving in ghostly silence, growing more and more
frantic, until in a bizarre rage she bites at her own
fingers. This sends* PERCY *off into laughter, but
alarms* MARTHA.)

MARTHA: Hey, you stop now.

(*She pulls* HELEN's *hand down.*)

You just sit quiet and—

(*But at once* HELEN *topples* MARTHA *on her back,
knees pinning her shoulders down, and grabs the
scissors.* MARTHA *screams.* PERCY *darts to the bell
string on the porch, yanks it, and the bell rings.*

*Inside, the lights have been gradually coming up
on the main room, where we see the family in-
formally gathered, talking, but in pantomime:* KATE
*sits darning socks near a cradle, occasionally rock-
ing it;* CAPTAIN KELLER *in spectacles is working over
newspaper pages at a table; a benign visitor in a
hat,* AUNT EV, *is sharing the sewing basket, putting
the finishing touches on a big shapeless doll made
out of towels; an indolent young man,* JAMES
KELLER, *is at the window watching the children.*

With the ring of the bell, KATE *is instantly on her
feet and out the door onto the porch, to take in
the scene; now we see what these five years have
done to her, the girlish playfulness is gone, she is
a woman steeled in grief.*)

KATE [FOR THE THOUSANDTH TIME]: Helen.

(*She is down the steps at once to them, seizing*
HELEN'S *wrists and lifting her off* MARTHA; MARTHA
runs off in tears and screams for momma, with
PERCY *after her.*)

Let me have those scissors.

(*Meanwhile the family inside is alerted,* AUNT EV
joining JAMES *at the window;* CAPTAIN KELLER *re-*
sumes work.)

JAMES [BLANDLY]: She only dug Martha's eyes out. Almost dug. It's always almost, no point worrying
till it happens, is there?

(*They gaze out, while* KATE *reaches for the scissors*
in HELEN'S *hand. But* HELEN *pulls the scissors back,*
they struggle for them a moment, then KATE *gives*
up, lets HELEN *keep them. She tries to draw* HELEN
into the house. HELEN *jerks away.* KATE *next goes*
down on her knees, takes HELEN'S *hands gently,*
and using the scissors like a doll, makes HELEN
caress and cradle them; she points HELEN'S *finger*
housewards. HELEN'S *whole body now becomes*
eager; she surrenders the scissors, KATE *turns her*
toward the door and gives her a little push. HELEN
scrambles up and toward the house, and KATE *ris-*
ing follows her.)

AUNT EV: How does she stand it? Why haven't you
seen this Baltimore man? It's not a thing you can
let go on and on, like the weather.

JAMES: The weather here doesn't ask permission of me, Aunt Ev. Speak to my father.

AUNT EV: Arthur. Something ought to be done for that child.

KELLER: A refreshing suggestion. What?

(KATE *entering turns* HELEN *to* AUNT EV, *who gives her the towel doll.*)

AUNT EV: Why, this very famous oculist in Baltimore I wrote you about, what was his name?

KATE: Dr. Chisholm.

AUNT EV: Yes, I heard lots of cases of blindness people thought couldn't be cured he's cured, he just does wonders. Why don't you write to him?

KELLER: I've stopped believing in wonders.

KATE [ROCKS THE CRADLE]: I think the Captain will write to him soon. Won't you, Captain?

KELLER: No.

JAMES [LIGHTLY]: Good money after bad, or bad after good. Or bad after bad—

AUNT EV: Well, if it's just a question of money, Arthur, now you're marshal you have this Yankee money. Might as well—

KELLER: Not money. The child's been to specialists all over Alabama and Tennessee, if I thought it would do good I'd have her to every fool doctor in the country.

KATE: I think the Captain will write to him soon.

KELLER: Katie. How many times can you let them break your heart?

KATE: Any number of times.

(HELEN *meanwhile sits on the floor to explore the doll with her fingers, and her hand pauses over the face: this is no face, a blank area of towel, and it troubles her. Her hand searches for features, and taps questioningly for eyes, but no one notices. She then yanks at her* AUNT'S *dress, and taps again vigorously for eyes.*)

AUNT EV: What, child?

(*Obviously not hearing,* HELEN *commences to go around, from person to person, tapping for eyes, but no one attends or understands.*)

KATE [NO BREAK]: As long as there's the least chance. For her to see. Or hear, or—

KELLER: There isn't. Now I must finish here.

KATE: I think, with your permission, Captain, I'd like to write.

KELLER: I said no, Katie.

AUNT EV: Why, writing does no harm, Arthur, only a little bitty letter. To see if he can help her.

KELLER: He can't.

KATE: We won't know that to be a fact, Captain, until after you write.

KELLER [RISING, EMPHATIC]: Katie, he can't.

(*He collects his papers.*)

JAMES [FACETIOUSLY]: Father stands up, that makes it a fact.

KELLER: You be quiet! I'm badgered enough here by females without your impudence.

(JAMES *shuts up, makes himself scarce.* HELEN *now is groping among things on* KELLER's *desk, and paws his papers to the floor.* KELLER *is exasperated.*)

Katie.

(KATE *quickly turns* HELEN *away, and retrieves the papers.*)

I might as well try to work in a henyard as in this house—

JAMES [PLACATING]: You really ought to put her away, Father.

KATE [STARING UP]: What?

JAMES: Some asylum. It's the kindest thing.

AUNT EV: Why, she's your sister, James, not a nobody—

JAMES: Half sister, and half—mentally defective, she can't even keep herself clean. It's not pleasant to see her about all the time.

KATE: Do you dare? Complain of what you *can* see?

KELLER [VERY ANNOYED]: This discussion is at an end! I'll thank you not to broach it again, Ev.

(*Silence descends at once.* HELEN *gropes her way with the doll, and* KELLER *turns back for a final word, explosive.*)

I've done as much as I can bear, I can't give my whole life to it! The house is at sixes and sevens from morning till night over the child, it's time some attention was paid to Mildred here instead!

KATE [GENTLY DRY]: You'll wake her up, Captain.

KELLER: I want some peace in the house, I don't care how, but one way we won't have it is by rushing up and down the country every time someone hears of a new quack. I'm as sensible to this affliction as anyone else, it hurts me to look at the girl.

KATE: It was not our affliction I meant you to write about, Captain.

(HELEN *is back at* AUNT EV, *fingering her dress, and yanks two buttons from it.*)

AUNT EV: Helen! My buttons.

(HELEN *pushes the buttons into the doll's face.* KATE *now sees, comes swiftly to kneel, lifts* HELEN'S *hand to her own eyes in question.*)

KATE: Eyes?

(HELEN *nods energetically.*)

She wants the doll to have eyes.

(*Another kind of silence now, while* KATE *takes pins and buttons from the sewing basket and attaches them to the doll as eyes.* KELLER *stands, caught, and watches morosely.* AUNT EV *blinks, and conceals her emotion by inspecting her dress.*)

AUNT EV: My goodness me, I'm not decent.

KATE: She doesn't know better, Aunt Ev. I'll sew them on again.

JAMES: Never learn with everyone letting her do anything she takes it into her mind to—

KELLER: You be quiet!

JAMES: What did I say now?

KELLER: You talk too much.

JAMES: I was agreeing with you!

KELLER: Whatever it was. Deprived child, the least she can have are the little things she wants.

(JAMES, *very wounded, stalks out of the room onto the porch; he remains here, sulking.*)

AUNT EV [INDULGENTLY]: It's worth a couple of buttons, Kate, look.

(HELEN *now has the doll with eyes, and cannot contain herself for joy; she rocks the doll, pats it vigorously, kisses it.*)

This child has more sense than all these men Kellers, if there's ever any way to reach that mind of hers.

(*But* HELEN *suddenly has come upon the cradle, and unhesitatingly overturns it; the swaddled baby tumbles out, and* CAPTAIN KELLER *barely manages to dive and catch it in time.*)

KELLER: *Helen!*

(*All are in commotion, the baby screams, but* HELEN *unperturbed is laying her doll in its place.* KATE *on her knees pulls her hands off the cradle, wringing them;* HELEN *is bewildered.*)

KATE: Helen, Helen, you're not to do such things, how can I make you understand—

KELLER [HOARSELY]: Katie.

KATE: How can I get it into your head, my darling, my poor—

KELLER: Katie, some way of teaching her an iota of discipline has to be—

KATE [FLARING]: How can you discipline an afflicted child? Is it her fault?

(HELEN's *fingers have fluttered to her* MOTHER's *lips, vainly trying to comprehend their movements.*)

KELLER: I didn't say it was her fault.

KATE: Then whose? I don't know what to do! How can I teach her, beat her—until she's black and blue?

KELLER: It's not safe to let her run around loose. Now there must be a way of confining her, somehow, so she can't—

KATE: Where, in a cage? She's a growing child, she has to use her limbs!

KELLER: Answer me one thing, is it fair to Mildred here?

KATE [INEXORABLY]: Are you willing to put her away?

(Now HELEN's *face darkens in the same rage as at herself earlier, and her hand strikes at* KATE's *lips.* KATE *catches her hand again, and* HELEN *begins to kick, struggle, twist.*)

KELLER: Now what?

KATE: She wants to talk, like—*be* like you and me.

(*She holds* HELEN *struggling until we hear from the child her first sound so far, an inarticulate weird noise in her throat such as an animal in a trap might make; and* KATE *releases her. The second she is free* HELEN *blunders away, collides violently with a chair, falls, and sits weeping.* KATE *comes to her, embraces, caresses, soothes her, and buries her own face in her hair, until she can control her voice.*)

Every day she slips further away. And I don't know how to call her back.

AUNT EV: Oh, I've a mind to take her up to Baltimore myself. If that doctor can't help her, maybe he'll know who can.

KELLER [PRESENTLY, HEAVILY]: I'll write the man, Katie.

(*He stands with the baby in his clasp, staring at* HELEN'S *head, hanging down on* KATE'S *arm.*

The lights dim out, except the one on KATE *and* HELEN. *In the twilight,* JAMES, AUNT EV, *and* KELLER *move off slowly, formally, in separate directions;* KATE *with* HELEN *in her arms remains, motionless, in an image which overlaps into the next scene and fades only when it is well under way.*

Without pause, from the dark down left we hear a man's voice with a Greek accent speaking:)

ANAGNOS: —who could do nothing for the girl, of course. It was Dr. Bell who thought she might somehow be taught. I have written the family only

that a suitable governess, Miss Annie Sullivan, has
been found here in Boston—

(*The lights begin to come up, down left, on a long
table and chair. The table contains equipment for
teaching the blind by touch—a small replica of
the human skeleton, stuffed animals, models of
flowers and plants, piles of books. The chair contains a girl of 20,* ANNIE SULLIVAN, *with a face
which in repose is grave and rather obstinate, and
when active is impudent, combative, twinkling
with all the life that is lacking in* HELEN'S, *and
handsome; there is a crude vitality to her. Her suitcase is at her knee.* ANAGNOS, *a stocky bearded
man, comes into the light only towards the end of
his speech.*)

ANAGNOS: —and will come. It will no doubt be difficult
for you there, Annie. But it has been difficult for
you at our school too, hm? Gratifying, yes, when
you came to us and could not spell your name, to
accomplish so much here in a few years, but always an Irish battle. For independence.

(*He studies* ANNIE, *humorously; she does not open
her eyes.*)

This is my last time to counsel you, Annie, and
you do lack some—by some I mean *all*—what,
tact or talent to bend. To others. And what has
saved you on more than one occasion here at Perkins is that there was nowhere to expel you to.
Your eyes hurt?

ANNIE: My ears, Mr. Anagnos.

(*And now she has opened her eyes; they are inflamed, vague, slightly crossed, clouded by the
granular growth of trachoma, and she often keeps
them closed to shut out the pain of light.*)

ANAGNOS [SEVERELY]: Nowhere but back to Tewksbury,
where children learn to be saucy. Annie, I know
how dreadful it was there, but that battle is dead
and done with, why not let it stay buried?

ANNIE [CHEERILY]: I think God must owe me a resurrection.

ANAGNOS [A BIT SHOCKED]: What?

ANNIE [TAPS HER BROW]: Well, He keeps digging up
that battle!

ANAGNOS: That is not a proper thing to say, Annie. It
is what I mean.

ANNIE [MEEKLY]: Yes. But I know what I'm like, what's
this child like?

ANAGNOS: Like?

ANNIE: Well— Bright or dull, to start off.

ANAGNOS: No one knows. And if she is dull, you have
no patience with this?

ANNIE: Oh, in grownups you have to, Mr. Anagnos. I
mean in children it just seems a little—precocious,
can I use that word?

ANAGNOS: Only if you can spell it.

ANNIE: Premature. So I hope at least she's a bright one.

ANAGNOS: Deaf, blind, mute—who knows? She is like a
little safe, locked, that no one can open. Perhaps
there is a treasure inside.

ANNIE: Maybe it's empty, too?

ANAGNOS: Possible. I should warn you, she is much given to tantrums.

ANNIE: Means something is inside. Well, so am I, if I believe all I hear. Maybe you should warn *them*.

ANAGNOS [FROWNS]: Annie. I wrote them no word of your history. You will find yourself among strangers now, who know nothing of it.

ANNIE: Well, we'll keep them in a state of blessed ignorance.

ANAGNOS: Perhaps *you* should tell it?

ANNIE [BRISTLING]: Why? I have enough trouble with people who don't know.

ANAGNOS: So they will understand. When you have trouble.

ANNIE: The only time I have trouble is when I'm right.

(*But she is amused at herself, as is* ANAGNOS.)

Is it my fault it's so often? I won't give them trouble, Mr. Anagnos, I'll be so ladylike they won't notice I've come.

ANAGNOS: Annie, be—humble. It is not as if you have so many offers to pick and choose. You will need their affection, working with this child.

ANNIE [HUMOROUSLY]: I hope I won't need their pity.

ANAGNOS: Oh, we can all use some pity.

(*Crisply*)

So. You are no longer our pupil, we throw you into the world, a teacher. *If* the child can be taught. No one expects you to work miracles, even for twenty-five dollars a month. Now, in this en-

velope a loan, for the railroad, which you will re-
pay me when you have a bank account. But in
this box, a gift. With our love.

(ANNIE *opens the small box he extends, and sees
a garnet ring. She looks up, blinking, and down.*)

I think other friends are ready to say goodbye.

(*He moves as though to open doors.*)

ANNIE: Mr. Anagnos.

(*Her voice is trembling.*)

Dear Mr. Anagnos, I—

(*But she swallows over getting the ring on her
finger, and cannot continue until she finds a woebegone joke.*)

Well, what should I say, I'm an ignorant opin-
ionated girl, and everything I am I owe to you?
ANAGNOS [SMILES]: That is only half true, Annie.
ANNIE: Which half? I crawled in here like a drowned
rat, I thought I died when Jimmie died, that I'd
never again—come alive. Well, you say with love
so easy, and I haven't *loved* a soul since and I
never will, I suppose, but this place gave me more
than my eyes back. Or taught me how to spell,
which I'll never learn anyway, but with all the
fights and the trouble I've been here it taught me
what help is, and how to live again, and I don't

want to say goodbye. Don't open the door, I'm
crying.

ANAGNOS [GENTLY]: They will not see.

(*He moves again as though opening doors, and in
comes a group of girls, 8-year-olds to 17-year-olds;
as they walk we see they are blind. ANAGNOS shepherds them in with a hand.*)

A CHILD: Annie?

ANNIE [HER VOICE CHEERFUL]: Here, Beatrice.

(*As soon as they locate her voice they throng joy-
fully to her, speaking all at once; ANNIE is down on
her knees to the smallest, and the following are
the more intelligible fragments in the general hub-
bub.*)

CHILDREN: There's a present. We brought you a going-
away present, Annie!

ANNIE: Oh, now you shouldn't have—

CHILDREN: We did, we did, where's the present?

SMALLEST CHILD [MOURNFULLY]: Don't go, Annie, away.

CHILDREN: Alice has it. Alice! Where's Alice? Here I
am! Where? Here!

(*An arm is aloft out of the group, waving a present; ANNIE reaches for it.*)

ANNIE. I have it. I have it, everybody, should I open it?

CHILDREN: Open it! Everyone be quiet! Do, Annie!
She's opening it. Ssh!

(A *settling of silence while* ANNIE *unwraps it. The present is a pair of smoked glasses, and she stands still.*)

Is it open, Annie?

ANNIE: It's open.

CHILDREN: It's for your eyes, Annie. Put them on, Annie! 'Cause Mrs. Hopkins said your eyes hurt since the operation. And she said you're going where the sun is *fierce.*

ANNIE: I'm putting them on now.

SMALLEST CHILD [MOURNFULLY]: Don't go, Annie, where the sun is fierce.

CHILDREN: Do they fit all right?

ANNIE: Oh, they fit just fine.

CHILDREN: Did you put them on? Are they pretty, Annie?

ANNIE: Oh, my eyes feel hundreds of per cent better already, and pretty, why, do you know how I look in them? Splendiloquent. Like a race horse!

CHILDREN [DELIGHTED]: There's another present! Beatrice! We have a present for Helen, too! Give it to her, Beatrice. Here, Annie!

(*This present is an elegant doll, with movable eyelids and a momma sound.*)

It's for Helen. And we took up a collection to buy it. And Laura dressed it.

ANNIE: It's beautiful!

CHILDREN: So don't forget, you be sure to give it to Helen from us, Annie!

ANNIE: I promise it will be the first thing I give her. If

I don't keep it for myself, that is, you know I
can't be trusted with dolls!

SMALLEST CHILD [MOURNFULLY]: Don't go, Annie, to
her.

ANNIE [HER ARM AROUND HER]: Sarah, dear. I don't
want to go.

SMALLEST CHILD: Then why are you going?

ANNIE [GENTLY]: Because I'm a big girl now, and big
girls have to earn a living. It's the only way I can.
But if you don't smile for me first, what I'll just
have to do is—

(*She pauses, inviting it.*)

SMALLEST CHILD: What?

ANNIE: Put *you* in my suitcase, instead of this doll. And
take *you* to Helen in Alabama!

(*This strikes the children as very funny, and they
begin to laugh and tease the smallest child, who
after a moment does smile for* ANNIE.)

ANAGNOS [THEN]: Come, children. We must get the
trunk into the carriage and Annie into her train,
or no one will go to Alabama. Come, come.

(*He shepherds them out and* ANNIE *is left alone
on her knees with the doll in her lap. She reaches
for her suitcase, and by a subtle change in the
color of the light, we go with her thoughts into
another time. We hear a boy's voice whispering;
perhaps we see shadowy intimations of these speak-
ers in the background.*)

BOY'S VOICE: Where we goin', Annie?

ANNIE [IN DREAD]: Jimmie.

BOY'S VOICE: Where we goin'?

ANNIE: I said—I'm takin' care of you—

BOY'S VOICE: Forever and ever?

MAN'S VOICE [IMPERSONAL]: Annie Sullivan, aged nine, virtually blind. James Sullivan, aged seven— What's the matter with your leg, Sonny?

ANNIE: Forever and ever.

MAN'S VOICE: Can't he walk without that crutch?

(ANNIE *shakes her head, and does not stop shaking it.*)

Girl goes to the women's ward. Boy to the men's.

BOY'S VOICE [IN TERROR]: Annie! Annie, don't let them take me—Annie!

ANAGNOS [OFFSTAGE]: Annie! Annie?

(*But this voice is real, in the present, and* ANNIE *comes up out of her horror, clearing her head with a final shake; the lights begin to pick out* KATE *in the* KELLER *house, as* ANNIE *in a bright tone calls back.*)

ANNIE: Coming!

(*This word catches* KATE, *who stands half turned and attentive to it, almost as though hearing it. Meanwhile* ANNIE *turns and hurries out, lugging the suitcase.*

The room dims out; the sound of railroad wheels

begins from off left, and maintains itself in a constant rhythm underneath the following scene; the remaining lights have come up on the KELLER *homestead.* JAMES *is lounging on the porch, waiting. In the upper bedroom which is to be* ANNIE'S, HELEN *is alone, puzzledly exploring, fingering and smelling things, the curtains, empty drawers in the bureau, water in the pitcher by the washbasin, fresh towels on the bedstead. Downstairs in the family room* KATE *turning to a mirror hastily adjusts her bonnet, watched by a Negro servant in an apron,* VINEY.)

VINEY: Let Mr. Jimmy go by hisself, you been pokin' that garden all day, you ought to rest your feet.

KATE: I can't wait to see her, Viney.

VINEY: Maybe she ain't gone be on this train neither.

KATE: Maybe she is.

VINEY: And maybe she ain't.

KATE: And maybe she is. Where's Helen?

VINEY: She upstairs, smellin' around. She know somethin' funny's goin' on.

KATE: Let her have her supper as soon as Mildred's in bed, and tell Captain Keller when he comes that we'll be delayed tonight.

VINEY: Again.

KATE: I don't think we need say *again.* Simply delayed will do.

(*She runs upstairs to* ANNIE'S *room,* VINEY *speaking after her.*)

VINEY: I mean that's what he gone say. "What, again?"

(VINEY *works at setting the table. Upstairs* KATE
stands in the doorway, watching HELEN'S *groping
explorations.*)

KATE: Yes, we're expecting someone. Someone for my
Helen.

(HELEN *happens upon her skirt, clutches her leg;*
KATE *in a tired dismay kneels to tidy her hair and
soiled pinafore.*)

Oh, dear, this was clean not an hour ago.

(HELEN *feels her bonnet, shakes her head darkly,
and tugs to get it off.* KATE *retains it with one hand,
diverts* HELEN *by opening her other hand under
her nose.*)

Here. For while I'm gone.

(HELEN *sniffs, reaches, and pops something into
her mouth, while* KATE *speaks a bit guiltily.*)

I don't think one peppermint drop will spoil your
supper.

(*She gives* HELEN *a quick kiss, evades her hands,
and hurries downstairs again. Meanwhile* CAPTAIN
KELLER *has entered the yard from around the rear
of the house, newspaper under arm, cleaning off
and munching on some radishes; he sees* JAMES
lounging at the porch post.)

KELLER: Jimmie?

JAMES [UNMOVING]: Sir?

KELLER [EYES HIM]: You don't look dressed for anything useful, boy.

JAMES: I'm not. It's for Miss Sullivan.

KELLER: Needn't keep holding up that porch, we have
wooden posts for that. I asked you to see that those
strawberry plants were moved this evening.

JAMES: I'm moving your—Mrs. Keller, instead. To the
station.

KELLER [HEAVILY]: Mrs. Keller. Must you always speak
of her as though you haven't met the lady?

(KATE *comes out on the porch, and* JAMES *inclines
his head.*)

JAMES [IRONIC]: Mother.

(*He starts off the porch, but sidesteps* KELLER'S
glare like a blow.)

I said mother!

KATE: Captain.

KELLER: Evening, my dear.

KATE: We're off to meet the train, Captain. Supper will
be a trifle delayed tonight.

KELLER: What, again?

KATE [BACKING OUT]: With your permission, Captain?

(*And they are gone.* KELLER *watches them offstage,
morosely.*

Upstairs HELEN *meanwhile has groped for her*

mother, touched her cheek in a meaningful gesture, waited, touched her cheek, waited, then
found the open door, and made her way down.
Now she comes into the family room, touches her
cheek again; VINEY regards her.)

VINEY: What you want, honey, your momma?

(HELEN *touches her cheek again.* VINEY *goes to the
sideboard, gets a tea-cake, gives it into* HELEN'S
hand; HELEN *pops it into her mouth.*)

Guess one little tea-cake ain't gone ruin your appetite.

(*She turns* HELEN *toward the door.* HELEN *wanders
out onto the porch, as* KELLER *comes up the steps.
Her hands encounter him, and she touches her
cheek again, waits.*)

KELLER: She's gone.

(*He is awkward with her; when he puts his hand
on her head, she pulls away.* KELLER *stands regard-
ing her, heavily.*)

She's gone, my son and I don't get along, you don't
know I'm your father, no one likes me, and supper's delayed.

(HELEN *touches her cheek, waits.* KELLER *fishes in
his pocket.*)

Here. I brought you some stick candy, one nibble
of sweets can't do any harm.

(*He gives her a large stick candy;* HELEN *falls to it.*
VINEY *peers out the window.*)

VINEY [REPROACHFULLY]: Cap'n Keller, now how'm I
gone get her to eat her supper you fill her up with
that trash?

KELLER [ROARS]: Tend to your work!

(VINEY *beats a rapid retreat.* KELLER *thinks better
of it, and tries to get the candy away from* HELEN,
but HELEN *hangs on to it; and when* KELLER *pulls,
she gives his leg a kick.* KELLER *hops about,* HELEN
*takes refuge with the candy down behind the
pump, and* KELLER *then irately flings his newspaper on the porch floor, stamps into the house past*
VINEY *and disappears.*

The lights half dim on the homestead, where VINEY
and HELEN *going about their business soon find
their way off. Meanwhile, the railroad sounds off
left have mounted in a crescendo to a climax typi-
cal of a depot at arrival time, the lights come up on
stage left, and we see a suggestion of a station.
Here* ANNIE *in her smoked glasses and disarrayed
by travel is waiting with her suitcase, while* JAMES
*walks to meet her; she has a battered paper-bound
book, which is a Perkins report, under her arm.*)

JAMES [COOLLY]: Miss Sullivan?

ANNIE [CHEERILY]: Here! At last, I've been on trains so
    many days I thought they must be backing up
    every time I dozed off—
JAMES: I'm James Keller.
ANNIE: James?

(*The name stops her.*)

I had a brother Jimmie. Are you Helen's?
JAMES: I'm only half a brother. You're to be her gov-
    erness?
ANNIE [LIGHTLY]: Well. Try!
JAMES [EYING HER]: You look like half a governess.

(KATE *enters.* ANNIE *stands moveless, while* JAMES
takes her suitcase. KATE'S *gaze on her is doubtful,
troubled.*)

Mrs. Keller, Miss Sullivan.

(KATE *takes her hand.*)

KATE [SIMPLY]: We've met every train for two days.

(ANNIE *looks at* KATE'S *face, and her good humor
comes back.*)

ANNIE: I changed trains every time they stopped, the
    man who sold me that ticket ought to be tied to
    the tracks—
JAMES: You have a trunk, Miss Sullivan?
ANNIE: Yes.

(She passes JAMES *a claim check, and he bears the suitcase out behind them.* ANNIE *holds the battered book.* KATE *is studying her face, and* ANNIE *returns the gaze; this is a mutual appraisal, southern gentlewoman and working-class Irish girl, and* ANNIE *is not quite comfortable under it.)*

You didn't bring Helen, I was hoping you would.
KATE: No, she's home.

(A pause. ANNIE *tries to make ladylike small talk, though her energy now and then erupts; she catches herself up whenever she hears it.)*

ANNIE: You—live far from town, Mrs. Keller?
KATE: Only a mile.
ANNIE: Well. I suppose I can wait one more mile. But don't be surprised if I get out to push the horse!
KATE: Helen's waiting for you, too. There's been such a bustle in the house, she expects something, heaven knows what.

(Now she voices part of her doubt, not as such, but ANNIE *understands it.)*

I expected—a desiccated spinster. You're very young.
ANNIE [RESOLUTELY]: Oh, you should have seen me when I left Boston. I got much older on this trip.
KATE: I mean, to teach anyone as difficult as Helen.
ANNIE: *I* mean to try. They can't put you in jail for trying!
KATE: Is it possible, even? To teach a deaf-blind child

half of what an ordinary child learns—has that
ever been done?

ANNIE: Half?

KATE: A tenth.

ANNIE [RELUCTANTLY]: No.

(KATE'S *face loses its remaining hope, still apprais-
ing her youth.*)

Dr. Howe did wonders, but—an ordinary child?
No, never. But then I thought when I was going
over his reports—

(*She indicates the one in her hand*)

—he never treated them like ordinary children.
More like—eggs everyone was afraid would break.

KATE [A PAUSE]: May I ask how old you are?

ANNIE: Well, I'm not in my teens, you know! I'm
twenty.

KATE: All of twenty.

(ANNIE *takes the bull by the horns, valiantly.*)

ANNIE: Mrs. Keller, don't lose heart just because I'm
not on my last legs. I have three big advantages
over Dr. Howe that money couldn't buy for you.
One is his work behind me, I've read every word he
wrote about it and he wasn't exactly what you'd
call a man of few words. Another is to *be* young,
why, I've got energy to do anything. The third is,
I've been blind.

(But it costs her something to say this.)

KATE [QUIETLY]: Advantages.
ANNIE [WRY]: Well, some have the luck of the Irish, some do not.

(KATE smiles; she likes her.)

KATE: What will you try to teach her first?
ANNIE: First, last, and—in between, language.
KATE: Language.
ANNIE: Language is to the mind more than light is to the eye. Dr. Howe said that.
KATE: Language.

(She shakes her head.)

We can't get through to teach her to sit still. You *are* young, despite your years, to have such—confidence. Do you, inside?

(ANNIE studies her face; she likes her, too.)

ANNIE: No, to tell you the truth I'm as shaky inside as a baby's rattle!

(They smile at each other, and KATE pats her hand.)

KATE: Don't be.

(JAMES returns to usher them off.)

We'll do all we can to help, and to make you feel
at home. Don't think of us as strangers, Miss
Annie.

ANNIE [CHEERILY]: Oh, strangers aren't so strange to me.
I've known them all my life!

(KATE *smiles again,* ANNIE *smiles back, and they
precede* JAMES *offstage.*

*The lights dim on them, having simultdneously
risen full on the house;* VINEY *has already entered
the family room, taken a water pitcher, and come
out and down to the pump. She pumps real water.
As she looks offstage, we hear the clop of hoofs, a
carriage stopping, and voices.*)

VINEY: Cap'n Keller! Cap'n Keller, they comin'!

(*She goes back into the house, as* KELLER *comes
out on the porch to gaze.*)

She sure 'nuff came, Cap'n.

(KELLER *descends, and crosses toward the carriage;
this conversation begins offstage and moves on.*)

KELLER [VERY COURTLY]: Welcome to Ivy Green, Miss
Sullivan. I take it you are Miss Sullivan—

KATE: My husband, Miss Annie, Captain Keller.

ANNIE [HER BEST BEHAVIOR]: Captain, how do you do.

KELLER: A pleasure to see you, at last. I trust you had
an agreeable journey?

ANNIE: Oh, I had several! When did this country get so big?

JAMES: Where would you like the trunk, father?

KELLER: Where Miss Sullivan can get at it, I imagine.

ANNIE: Yes, please. Where's Helen?

KELLER: In the hall, Jimmie—

KATE: We've put you in the upstairs corner room, Miss Annie, if there's any breeze at all this summer, you'll feel it—

(*In the house the setter* BELLE *flees into the family room, pursued by* HELEN *with groping hands; the dog doubles back out the same door, and* HELEN *still groping for her makes her way out to the porch; she is messy, her hair tumbled, her pinafore now ripped, her shoelaces untied.* KELLER *acquires the suitcase, and* ANNIE *gets her hands on it too, though still endeavoring to live up to the general air of propertied manners.*)

KELLER: And the suitcase—

ANNIE [PLEASANTLY]:I'll take the suitcase, thanks.

KELLER: Not at all, I have it, Miss Sullivan.

ANNIE: I'd like it.

KELLER [GALLANTLY]: I couldn't think of it, Miss Sullivan. You'll find in the south we—

ANNIE: Let me.

KELLER: —view women as the flowers of civiliza—

ANNIE [IMPATIENTLY]: I've got something in it for Helen!

(*She tugs it free;* KELLER *stares.*)

Thank you. When do I see her?

KATE: There. There is Helen.

(ANNIE *turns, and sees* HELEN *on the porch. A moment of silence. Then* ANNIE *begins across the yard to her, lugging her suitcase.*)

KELLER [SOTTO VOCE]: Katie—

(KATE *silences him with a hand on his arm. When* ANNIE *finally reaches the porch steps she stops, contemplating* HELEN *for a last moment before entering her world. Then she drops the suitcase on the porch with intentional heaviness,* HELEN *starts with the jar, and comes to grope over it.* ANNIE *puts forth her hand, and touches* HELEN'S. HELEN *at once grasps it, and commences to explore it, like reading a face. She moves her hand on to* ANNIE'S *forearm, and dress; and* ANNIE *brings her face within reach of* HELEN'S *fingers, which travel over it, quite without timidity, until they encounter and push aside the smoked glasses.* ANNIE'S *gaze is grave, unpitying, very attentive. She puts her hands on* HELEN'S *arms, but* HELEN *at once pulls away, and they confront each other with a distance between. Then* HELEN *returns to the suitcase, tries to open it, cannot.* ANNIE *points* HELEN'S *hand overhead.* HELEN *pulls away, tries to open the suitcase again;* ANNIE *points her hand overhead again.* HELEN *points overhead, a question, and* ANNIE, *drawing* HELEN'S *hand to her own face, nods.* HELEN *now begins tugging the suitcase toward the door; when* ANNIE *tries to take it from her, she fights her off and backs through the doorway with it.* ANNIE *stands a moment, then fol-*

lows her in, and together they get the suitcase up
the steps into ANNIE'S *room.*)

KATE: Well?

KELLER: She's very rough, Katie.

KATE: I like her, Captain.

KELLER: Certainly rear a peculiar kind of young woman
in the north. How old is she?

KATE [VAGUELY]: Ohh— Well, she's not in her teens,
you know.

KELLER: She's only a child. What's her family like,
shipping her off alone this far?

KATE: I couldn't learn. She's very closemouthed about
some things.

KELLER: Why does she wear those glasses? I like to see
a person's eyes when I talk to—

KATE: For the sun. She was blind.

KELLER: Blind.

KATE: She's had nine operations on her eyes. One just
before she left.

KELLER: Blind, good heavens, do they expect one blind
child to teach another? Has she experience at least,
how long did she teach there?

KATE: She was a pupil.

KELLER [HEAVILY]: Katie, Katie. This is her first position?

KATE [BRIGHT VOICE]: She was valedictorian—

KELLER: Here's a houseful of grownups can't cope with
the child, how can an inexperienced half-blind
Yankee schoolgirl manage her?

(JAMES *moves in with the trunk on his shoulder.*)

JAMES [EASILY]: Great improvement. Now we have two of them to look after.

KELLER: You look after those strawberry plants!

(JAMES *stops with the trunk.* KELLER *turns from him without another word, and marches off.*)

JAMES: Nothing I say is right.

KATE: Why say anything?

(*She calls.*)

Don't be long, Captain, we'll have supper right away—

(*She goes into the house, and through the rear door of the family room.* JAMES *trudges in with the trunk, takes it up the steps to* ANNIE's *room, and sets it down outside the door. The lights elsewhere dim somewhat.*

Meanwhile, inside, ANNIE *has given* HELEN *a key; while* ANNIE *removes her bonnet,* HELEN *unlocks and opens the suitcase. The first thing she pulls out is a voluminous shawl. She fingers it until she perceives what it is; then she wraps it around her, and acquiring* ANNIE's *bonnet and smoked glasses as well, dons the lot: the shawl swamps her, and the bonnet settles down upon the glasses, but she stands before a mirror cocking her head to one side, then to the other, in a mockery of adult action.* ANNIE *is amused, and talks to her as one might to a kitten, with no trace of company manners.*)

ANNIE: All the trouble I went to and that's how I look?

(HELEN *then comes back to the suitcase, gropes for more, lifts out a pair of female drawers.*)

Oh, no. Not the drawers!

(*But* HELEN *discarding them comes to the elegant doll. Her fingers explore its features, and when she raises it and finds its eyes open and close, she is at first startled, then delighted. She picks it up, taps its head vigorously, taps her own chest, and nods questioningly.* ANNIE *takes her finger, points it to the doll, points it to* HELEN, *and touching it to her own face, also nods.* HELEN *sits back on her heels, clasps the doll to herself, and rocks it.* ANNIE *studies her, still in bonnet and smoked glasses like a caricature of herself, and addresses her humorously.*)

All right, Miss O'Sullivan. Let's begin with doll.

(*She takes* HELEN's *hand; in her palm* ANNIE's *forefinger points, thumb holding her other fingers clenched.*)

D.

(*Her thumb next holds all her fingers clenched, touching* HELEN's *palm.*)

O.

(*Her thumb and forefinger extend.*)

L.

(*Same contact repeated.*)

L.

(*She puts* HELEN's *hand to the doll.*)

Doll.

JAMES: You spell pretty well.

(ANNIE *in one hurried move gets the drawers
swiftly back into the suitcase, the lid banged shut,
and her head turned, to see* JAMES *leaning in the
doorway.*)

Finding out if she's ticklish? She is.

(ANNIE *regards him stonily, but* HELEN *after a
scowling moment tugs at her hand again, imperious.* ANNIE *repeats the letters, and* HELEN *interrupts
her fingers in the middle, feeling each of them,
puzzled.* ANNIE *touches* HELEN's *hand to the doll,
and begins spelling into it again.*)

JAMES: What is it, a game?
ANNIE [CURTLY]: An alphabet.
JAMES: Alphabet?
ANNIE: For the deaf.

(HELEN *now repeats the finger movements in air,
exactly, her head cocked to her own hand, and
*ANNIE's *eyes suddenly gleam.*)

Ho. How *bright* she is!

JAMES: You think she knows what she's doing?

(*He takes* HELEN'*s hand, to throw a meaningless gesture into it; she repeats this one too.*)

She imitates everything, she's a monkey.

ANNIE [VERY PLEASED]: Yes, she's a bright little monkey, all right.

(*She takes the doll from* HELEN, *and reaches for her hand;* HELEN *instantly grabs the doll back.* ANNIE *takes it again, and* HELEN'*s hand next, but* HELEN *is incensed now; when* ANNIE *draws her hand to her face to shake her head no, then tries to spell to her,* HELEN *slaps at* ANNIE'*s face.* ANNIE *grasps* HELEN *by both arms, and swings her into a chair, holding her pinned there, kicking, while glasses, doll, bonnet fly in various directions.* JAMES *laughs.*)

JAMES: She wants her doll back.

ANNIE: When she spells it.

JAMES: Spell, she doesn't know the thing has a name, even.

ANNIE: Of course not, who expects her to, now? All I want is her fingers to learn the letters.

JAMES: Won't mean anything to her.

(ANNIE *gives him a look. She then tries to form* HELEN'*s fingers into the letters, but* HELEN *swings a haymaker instead, which* ANNIE *barely ducks, at once pinning her down again.*)

Doesn't like that alphabet, Miss Sullivan. You invent it yourself?

(HELEN *is now in a rage, fighting tooth and nail to get out of the chair, and* ANNIE *answers while struggling and dodging her kicks.*)

ANNIE: Spanish monks under a—vow of silence. Which I wish *you'd* take!

(*And suddenly releasing* HELEN's *hands, she comes and shuts the door in* JAMES' *face.* HELEN *drops to the floor, groping around for the doll.* ANNIE *looks around desperately, sees her purse on the bed, rummages in it, and comes up with a battered piece of cake wrapped in newspaper; with her foot she moves the doll deftly out of the way of* HELEN's *groping, and going on her knee she lets* HELEN *smell the cake. When* HELEN *grabs for it,* ANNIE *removes the cake and spells quickly into the reaching hand.*)

Cake. From Washington up north, it's the best I can do.

(HELEN's *hand waits, baffled.* ANNIE *repeats it.*)

C, a, k, e. Do what my fingers do, never mind what it means.

(*She touches the cake briefly to* HELEN's *nose, pats her hand, presents her own hand.* HELEN *spells the letters rapidly back.* ANNIE *pats her hand enthusias-*

tically, and gives her the cake; HELEN *crams it into her mouth with both hands.* ANNIE *watches her, with humor.)*

Get it down fast, maybe I'll steal that back too. Now.

(She takes the doll, touches it to HELEN'S *nose, and spells again into her hand.)*

D, o, l, l. Think it over.

*(*HELEN *thinks it over, while* ANNIE *presents her own hand. Then* HELEN *spells three letters.* ANNIE *waits a second, then completes the word for* HELEN *in her palm.)*

L.

(She hands over the doll, and HELEN *gets a good grip on its leg.)*

Imitate now, understand later. End of the first les—

(She never finishes, because HELEN *swings the doll with a furious energy, it hits* ANNIE *squarely in the face, and she falls back with a cry of pain, her knuckles up to her mouth.* HELEN *waits, tensed for further combat. When* ANNIE *lowers her knuckles she looks at blood on them; she works her lips, gets to her feet, finds the mirror, and bares her teeth at herself. Now she is furious herself.)*

You little wretch, no one's taught you *any* manners? I'll—

*(But rounding from the mirror she sees the door
slam,* HELEN *and the doll are on the outside, and*
HELEN *is turning the key in the lock.* ANNIE *darts
over, to pull the knob; the door is locked fast. She
yanks it again.)*

Helen! Helen, let me out of—

(She bats her brow at the folly of speaking, but
JAMES, *now downstairs, hears her and turns to see*
HELEN *with the key and doll groping her way down
the steps;* JAMES *takes in the whole situation,
makes a move to intercept* HELEN, *but then changes
his mind, lets her pass, and amusedly follows her
out onto the porch. Upstairs* ANNIE *meanwhile
rattles the knob, kneels, peers through the keyhole,
gets up. She goes to the window, looks down,
frowns.* JAMES *from the yard sings gaily up to her:)*

JAMES:

    Buffalo girl, are you coming out tonight,
    Coming out tonight,
    Coming out—

(He drifts back into the house. ANNIE *takes a handkerchief, nurses her mouth, stands in the middle of
the room, staring at door and window in turn, and
so catches sight of herself in the mirror, her cheek
scratched, her hair dishevelled, her handkerchief*

*bloody, her face disgusted with herself. She ad-
dresses the mirror, with some irony.)*

ANNIE: Don't worry. They'll find you, you're not lost.
Only out of place.

*(But she coughs, spits something into her palm,
and stares at it, outraged.)*

And toothless.

(She winces.)

Oo! It hurts.

*(She pours some water into the basin, dips the
handkerchief, and presses it to her mouth. Standing there, bent over the basin in pain—with the
rest of the set dim and unreal, and the lights upon
her taking on the subtle color of the past—she
hears again, as do we, the faraway voices, and
slowly she lifts her head to them; the boy's voice
is the same, the others are cracked old crones in a
nightmare, and perhaps we see their shadows.)*

BOY'S VOICE: It hurts. Annie, it hurts.
FIRST CRONE'S VOICE: Keep that brat shut up, can't you,
girlie, how's a body to get any sleep in this damn
ward?
BOY'S VOICE: It hurts. It hurts.
SECOND CRONE'S VOICE: Shut up, you!
BOY'S VOICE: Annie, when are we goin' home? You
promised!

ANNIE: Jimmie—

BOY'S VOICE: Forever and ever, you said forever—

(ANNIE *drops the handkerchief, averts to the window, and is arrested there by the next cry.*)

Annie? Annie, you there? Annie! It *hurts!*

THIRD CRONE'S VOICE: Grab him, he's fallin'!

BOY'S VOICE: *Annie!*

DOCTOR'S VOICE [A PAUSE, SLOWLY]: Little girl. Little girl, I must tell you your brother will be going on a—

(But ANNIE *claps her hands to her ears, to shut this out; there is instant silence.*

As the lights bring the other areas in again, JAMES *goes to the steps to listen for any sound from upstairs.* KELLER *re-entering from left crosses toward the house; he passes* HELEN *en route to her retreat under the pump.* KATE *re-enters the rear door of the family room, with flowers for the table.*)

KATE: Supper is ready, Jimmie, will you call your father?

JAMES: Certainly.

(*But he calls up the stairs, for* ANNIE's *benefit:*)

Father! Supper!

KELLER [AT THE DOOR]: No need to shout, I've been cooling my heels for an hour. Sit down.

JAMES: Certainly.

KELLER: Viney!

(VINEY *backs in with a roast, while they get settled around the table.*)

VINEY: Yes, Cap'n, right here.

KATE: Mildred went directly to sleep, Viney?

VINEY: Oh yes, that babe's a angel.

KATE: And Helen had a good supper?

VINEY [VAGUELY]: I dunno, Miss Kate, somehow she didn't have much of a appetite tonight—

KATE [A BIT GUILTY]: Oh. Dear.

KELLER [HASTILY]: Well, now. Couldn't say the same for my part, I'm famished. Katie, your plate.

KATE [LOOKING]: But where is Miss Annie?

(A *silence.*)

JAMES [PLEASANTLY]: In her room.

KELLER: In her room? Doesn't she know hot food must be eaten hot? Go bring her down at once, Jimmie.

JAMES [RISES]: Certainly. I'll get a ladder.

KELLER [STARES]: What?

JAMES: I'll need a ladder. Shouldn't take me long.

KATE [STARES]: What shouldn't take you—

KELLER: Jimmie, do as I say! Go upstairs at once and tell Miss Sullivan supper is getting cold—

JAMES: She's locked in her room.

KELLER: Locked in her—

KATE: What on earth are you—

JAMES: Helen locked her in and made off with the key.

KATE [RISING]: And you sit here and say nothing?

JAMES: Well, everyone's been telling me not to say anything.

(*He goes serenely out and across the yard, whistling.* KELLER *thrusting up from his chair makes for
the stairs.*)

KATE: Viney, look out in back for Helen. See if she has
that key.

VINEY: Yes, Miss Kate.

(VINEY *goes out the rear door.*)

KELLER [CALLING DOWN]: She's out by the pump!

(KATE *goes out on the porch after* HELEN, *while*
KELLER *knocks on* ANNIE'S *door, then rattles the
knob, imperiously.*)

Miss Sullivan! Are you in there?

ANNIE: Oh, I'm in here, all right.

KELLER: Is there no key on your side?

ANNIE [WITH SOME ASPERITY]: Well, if there was a key
in here, *I* wouldn't be in here. Helen took it, the
only thing on my side is me.

KELLER: Miss Sullivan. I—

(*He tries, but cannot hold it back.*)

Not in the house ten minutes, I don't see *how* you
managed it!

(*He stomps downstairs again, while* ANNIE *mutters
to herself.*)

ANNIE: And even I'm not on my side.

KELLER [ROARING]: Viney!

VINEY [REAPPEARING]: Yes, Cap'n?

KELLER: Put that meat back in the oven!

> (VINEY *bears the roast off again, while* KELLER *strides out onto the porch.* KATE *is with* HELEN *at the pump, opening her hands.*)

KATE: She has no key.

KELLER: Nonsense, she must have the key. Have you searched in her pockets?

KATE: Yes. She doesn't have it.

KELLER: Katie, she must have the key.

KATE: Would you prefer to search her yourself, Captain?

KELLER: No, I would not prefer to search her! She almost took my kneecap off this evening, when I tried merely to—

> (JAMES *reappears carrying a long ladder, with* PERCY *running after him to be in on things.*)

Take that ladder back!

JAMES: Certainly.

> (*He turns around with it.* MARTHA *comes skipping around the upstage corner of the house to be in on things, accompanied by the setter* BELLE.)

KATE: She could have hidden the key.

KELLER: Where?

KATE: Anywhere. Under a stone. In the flower beds. In
the grass—

KELLER: Well, I can't plow up the entire grounds to
find a missing key! Jimmie!

JAMES: Sir?

KELLER: Bring me a ladder!

JAMES: Certainly.

(VINEY *comes around the downstage side of the*
house to be in on things; she has MILDRED *over her*
shoulder, bleating. KELLER *places the ladder against*
ANNIE's *window and mounts.* ANNIE *meanwhile is*
running about making herself presentable, washing
the blood off her mouth, straightening her clothes,
tidying her hair. Another Negro servant enters to
gaze in wonder, increasing the gathering ring of
spectators.)

KATE [SHARPLY]: What is Mildred doing up?

VINEY: Cap'n woke her, ma'am, all that hollerin'.

KELLER: Miss Sullivan!

(ANNIE *comes to the window, with as much air of*
gracious normality as she can manage; KELLER *is*
at the window.)

ANNIE [BRIGHTLY]: Yes, Captain Keller?

KELLER: Come out!

ANNIE: I don't see how I can. There isn't room.

KELLER: I intend to carry you. Climb onto my shoulder
and hold tight.

ANNIE: Oh, no. It's—very chivalrous of you, but I'd
really prefer to—

KELLER: Miss Sullivan, follow instructions! I will not
have you also tumbling out of our windows.

(ANNIE *obeys, with some misgivings.*)

I hope this is not a sample of what we may expect
from you. In the way of simplifying the work of
looking after Helen.

ANNIE: Captain Keller, I'm perfectly able to go down a
ladder under my own—

KELLER: I doubt it, Miss Sullivan. Simply hold onto my
neck.

(*He begins down with her, while the spectators
stand in a wide and somewhat awe-stricken circle,
watching.* KELLER *half-misses a rung, and* ANNIE
grabs at his whiskers.)

My *neck*, Miss Sullivan!

ANNIE: I'm sorry to inconvenience you this way—

KELLER: No inconvenience, other than having that door
taken down and the lock replaced, if we fail to find
that key.

ANNIE: Oh, I'll look everywhere for it.

KELLER: Thank you. Do not look in any rooms that can
be locked. There.

(*He stands her on the ground.* JAMES *applauds.*)

ANNIE: Thank you very much.

(*She smooths her skirt, looking as composed and
ladylike as possible.* KELLER *stares around at the
spectators.*)

KELLER: Go, go, back to your work. What are you looking at here? There's nothing here to look at.

(*They break up, move off.*)

Now would it be possible for us to have supper, like other people?

(*He marches into the house.*)

KATE: Viney, serve supper. I'll put Mildred to sleep.

(*They all go in.* JAMES *is the last to leave, murmuring to* ANNIE *with a gesture.*)

JAMES: Might as well leave the l, a, d, d, e, r, hm?

(ANNIE *ignores him, looking at* HELEN; JAMES *goes in too. Imperceptibly the lights commence to narrow down.* ANNIE *and* HELEN *are now alone in the yard,* HELEN *seated at the pump, where she has been oblivious to it all, a battered little savage, playing with the doll in a picture of innocent contentment.* ANNIE *comes near, leans against the house, and taking off her smoked glasses, studies her, not without awe. Presently* HELEN *rises, gropes around to see if anyone is present;* ANNIE *evades her hand, and when* HELEN *is satisfied she is alone, the key suddenly protrudes out of her mouth. She takes it in her fingers, stands thinking, gropes to the pump, lifts a loose board, drops the key into the well, and hugs herself gleefully.* ANNIE *stares. But*

after a moment she shakes her head to herself, she
cannot keep the smile from her lips.)

ANNIE: You *devil.*

(Her tone is one of great respect, humor, and ac-
ceptance of challenge.)

You think I'm so easily gotten rid of? You have a
thing or two to learn, first. I have nothing else to
do.

(She goes up the steps to the porch, but turns for
a final word, almost of warning.)

And nowhere to go.

(And presently she moves into the house to the
others, as the lights dim down and out, except for
the small circle upon HELEN *solitary at the pump,*
which ends the act.)

ACT II

The only room visible in the KELLER *house is* ANNIE'S, *where by lamplight* ANNIE *in a shawl is at a desk writing a letter; at her bureau* HELEN *in her customary unkempt state is tucking her doll in the bottom drawer as a cradle, the contents of which she has dumped out, creating as usual a fine disorder.*

ANNIE *mutters each word as she writes her letter, slowly, her eyes close to and almost touching the page, to follow with difficulty her penwork.*

ANNIE: ". . . and, nobody, here, has, attempted, to, control, her. The, greatest, problem, I, have, is, how, to, disipline, her, without, breaking, her, spirit."

   (*Resolute voice*)

   "But, I, shall, insist, on, reasonable, obedience, from, the, start—"

   (*At which point* HELEN, *groping about on the desk, knocks over the inkwell.* ANNIE *jumps up, rescues her letter, rights the inkwell, grabs a towel to stem the spillage, and then wipes at* HELEN'S *hands;* HELEN *as always pulls free, but 'not until* ANNIE *first gets three letters into her palm.*)

Ink.

(HELEN *is enough interested in and puzzled by this spelling that she proffers her hand again; so* ANNIE *spells and impassively dunks it back in the spillage.*)

Ink. It has a name.

(*She wipes the hand clean, and leads* HELEN *to her bureau, where she looks for something to engage her. She finds a sewing card, with needle and thread, and going to her knees, shows* HELEN'S *hand how to connect one row of holes.*)

Down. Under. Up. And be careful of the needle—

(HELEN *gets it, and* ANNIE *rises.*)

Fine. You keep out of the ink and perhaps I can keep out of—the soup.

(*She returns to the desk, tidies it, and resumes writing her letter, bent close to the page.*)

"These, blots, are, her, handiwork. I—"

(*She is interrupted by a gasp:* HELEN *has stuck her finger, and sits sucking at it, darkly. Then with vengeful resolve she seizes her doll, and is about to dash its brains out on the floor when* ANNIE *diving catches it in one hand, which she at once shakes with hopping pain but otherwise ignores, patiently.)*

All right, let's try temperance.

(Taking the doll, she kneels, goes through the motion of knocking its head on the floor, spells into HELEN's *hand:)*

Bad, girl.

(She lets HELEN *feel the grieved expression on her face.* HELEN *imitates it. Next she makes* HELEN *caress the doll and kiss the hurt spot and hold it gently in her arms, then spells into her hand:)*

Good, girl.

(She lets HELEN *feel the smile on her face.* HELEN *sits with a scowl, which suddenly clears; she pats the doll, kisses it, wreathes her face in a large artificial smile, and bears the doll to the washstand, where she carefully sits it.* ANNIE *watches, pleased.)*

Very good girl—

(Whereupon HELEN *elevates the pitcher and dashes it on the floor instead.* ANNIE *leaps to her feet, and stands inarticulate;* HELEN *calmly gropes back to sit to the sewing card and needle.*

ANNIE *manages to achieve self-control. She picks up a fragment or two of the pitcher, sees* HELEN *is*

*puzzling over the card, and resolutely kneels to
demonstrate it again. She spells into* HELEN's *hand.*

KATE *meanwhile coming around the corner with
folded sheets on her arm, halts at the doorway and
watches them for a moment in silence; she is
moved, but level.*)

KATE [PRESENTLY]: What are you saying to her?

(ANNIE *glancing up is a bit embarrassed, and rises
from the spelling, to find her company manners.*)

ANNIE: Oh, I was just making conversation. Saying it
was a sewing card.
KATE: But does that—

(*She imitates with her fingers*)

—mean that to her?
ANNIE: No. No, she won't know what spelling is till she
knows what a word is.
KATE: Yet you keep spelling to her. Why?
ANNIE [CHEERILY]: I like to hear myself talk!
KATE: The Captain says it's like spelling to the fence
post.
ANNIE [A PAUSE]: Does he, now.
KATE: Is it?
ANNIE: No, it's how I watch you talk to Mildred.
KATE: Mildred.
ANNIE: Any baby. Gibberish, grown-up gibberish, baby-
talk gibberish, do they understand one word of it
to start? Somehow they begin to. If they hear it,
I'm letting Helen hear it.

KATE: Other children are not—impaired.

ANNIE: Ho, there's nothing impaired in that head, it works like a mousetrap!

KATE [SMILES]: But after a child hears how many words, Miss Annie, a million?

ANNIE: I guess no mother's ever minded enough to count.

(*She drops her eyes to spell into* HELEN'S *hand, again indicating the card;* HELEN *spells back, and* ANNIE *is amused.*)

KATE [TOO QUICKLY]: What did she spell?

ANNIE: I spelt card. She spelt cake!

(*She takes in* KATE'S *quickness, and shakes her head, gently.*)

No, it's only a finger-game to her, Mrs. Keller. What she has to learn first is that things have names.

KATE: And when will she learn?

ANNIE: Maybe after a million and one words.

(*They hold each other's gaze;* KATE *then speaks quietly.*)

KATE: I should like to learn those letters, Miss Annie.

ANNIE [PLEASED]: I'll teach you tomorrow morning. That makes only half a million each!

KATE [THEN]: It's her bedtime.

(ANNIE *reaches for the sewing card,* HELEN *objects,* ANNIE *insists, and* HELEN *gets rid of* ANNIE'S *hand*

by jabbing it with the needle. ANNIE *gasps, and
moves to grip* HELEN'S *wrist; but* KATE *intervenes
with a proffered sweet, and* HELEN *drops the card,
crams the sweet into her mouth, and scrambles up
to search her mother's hands for more.* ANNIE
nurses her wound, staring after the sweet.)

I'm sorry, Miss Annie.

ANNIE [INDIGNANTLY]: Why does she get a reward? For
stabbing me?

KATE: Well—

(*Then, tiredly*)

We catch our flies with honey, I'm afraid. We
haven't the heart for much else, and so many
times she simply cannot be compelled.

ANNIE [OMINOUS]: Yes. I'm the same way myself.

(KATE *smiles, and leads* HELEN *off around the
corner.* ANNIE *alone in her room picks up things
and in the act of removing* HELEN'S *doll gives way
to unmannerly temptation: she throttles it. She
drops it on her bed, and stands pondering. Then
she turns back, sits decisively, and writes again, as
the lights dim on her.*)

(*Grimly*)

"The, more, I, think, the, more, certain, I, am,
that, obedience, is, the, gateway, through, which,
knowledge, enters, the, mind, of, the, child—"

(*On the word "obedience" a shaft of sunlight hits the water pump outside, while* ANNIE'S *voice ends in the dark, followed by a distant cockcrow; daylight comes up over another corner of the sky, with* VINEY'S *voice heard at once.*)

VINEY: Breakfast ready!

(VINEY *comes down into the sunlight beam, and pumps a pitcherful of water. While the pitcher is brimming we hear conversation from the dark; the light grows to the family room of the house where all are either entering or already seated at breakfast, with* KELLER *and* JAMES *arguing the war.* HELEN *is wandering around the table to explore the contents of the other plates. When* ANNIE *is in her chair, she watches* HELEN. VINEY *re-enters, sets the pitcher on the table;* KATE *lifts the almost empty biscuit plate with an inquiring look,* VINEY *nods and bears it off back, neither of them interrupting the men.* ANNIE *meanwhile sits with fork quiet, watching* HELEN, *who at her mother's plate pokes her hand among some scrambled eggs.* KATE *catches* ANNIE'S *eyes on her, smiles with a wry gesture.* HELEN *moves on to* JAMES'S *plate, the male talk continuing,* JAMES *deferential and* KELLER *overriding.*)

JAMES: —no, but shouldn't we give the devil his due, father? The fact is we lost the South two years earlier when he outthought us behind Vicksburg.

KELLER: Outthought is a peculiar word for a butcher.

JAMES: Harness maker, wasn't he?

KELLER: I said butcher, his only virtue as a soldier was numbers and he led them to slaughter with no more regard than for so many sheep.

JAMES: But even if in that sense he was a butcher, the fact is he—

KELLER: And a drunken one, half the war.

JAMES: Agreed, father. If his own people said he was I can't argue he—

KELLER: Well, what is it you find to admire in such a man, Jimmie, the butchery or the drunkenness?

JAMES: Neither, father, only the fact that he beat us.

KELLER: He didn't.

JAMES: Is it your contention we won the war, sir?

KELLER: He didn't beat us at Vicksburg. We lost Vicksburg because Pemberton gave Bragg five thousand of his cavalry and Loring, whom I knew personally for a nincompoop before you were born, marched away from Champion's Hill with enough men to have held them, we lost Vicksburg by stupidity verging on treason.

JAMES: I would have said we lost Vicksburg because Grant was one thing no Yankee general was before him—

KELLER: Drunk? I doubt it.

JAMES: Obstinate.

KELLER: Obstinate. Could any of them compare even in that with old Stonewall? If he'd been there we would still have Vicksburg.

JAMES: Well, the butcher simply wouldn't give up, he tried four ways of getting around Vicksburg and on the fifth try he got around. Anyone else would have pulled north and—

KELLER: He wouldn't have got around if we'd had a Southerner in command, instead of a half-breed Yankee traitor like Pemberton—

(*While this background talk is in progress,* HELEN *is working around the table, ultimately toward* ANNIE'S *plate. She messes with her hands in* JAMES'S *plate, then in* KELLER'S, *both men taking it so for granted they hardly notice. Then* HELEN *comes groping with soiled hands past her own plate, to* ANNIE'S; *her hand goes to it, and* ANNIE, *who has been waiting, deliberately lifts and removes her hand.* HELEN *gropes again,* ANNIE *firmly pins her by the wrist, and removes her hand from the table.* HELEN *thrusts her hands again,* ANNIE *catches them, and* HELEN *begins to flail and make noises; the interruption brings* KELLER'S *gaze upon them.*)

What's the matter there?
KATE: Miss Annie. You see, she's accustomed to helping herself from our plates to anything she—
ANNIE [EVENLY]: Yes, but *I'm* not accustomed to it.
KELLER: No, of course not. Viney!
KATE: Give her something, Jimmie, to quiet her.
JAMES [BLANDLY]: But her table manners are the best she has. Well.

(*He pokes across with a chunk of bacon at* HELEN'S *hand, which* ANNIE *releases; but* HELEN *knocks the bacon away and stubbornly thrusts at* ANNIE'S *plate,* ANNIE *grips her wrists again, the struggle mounts.*)

KELLER: Let her this time, Miss Sullivan, it's the only way we get any adult conversation. If my son's half merits that description.

(*He rises.*)

I'll get you another plate.

ANNIE [GRIPPING HELEN]: I have a plate, thank you.

KATE [CALLING]: Viney! I'm afraid what Captain Keller says is only too true, she'll persist in this until she gets her own way.

KELLER [AT THE DOOR]: Viney, bring Miss Sullivan another plate—

ANNIE [STONILY]: I have a plate, nothing's wrong with the *plate*, I intend to keep it.

(*Silence for a moment, except for* HELEN's *noises as she struggles to get loose; the* KELLERS *are a bit nonplussed, and* ANNIE *is too darkly intent on* HELEN's *manners to have any thoughts now of her own.*)

JAMES: Ha. You see why they took Vicksburg?

KELLER [UNCERTAINLY]: Miss Sullivan. One plate or another is hardly a matter to struggle with a deprived child about.

ANNIE: Oh, I'd sooner have a more—

(HELEN *begins to kick,* ANNIE *moves her ankles to the opposite side of the chair.*)

—heroic issue myself, I—

KELLER: No, I really must insist you—

(HELEN *bangs her toe on the chair and sinks to the
floor, crying with rage and feigned injury;* ANNIE
keeps hold of her wrists, gazing down, while KATE
rises.)

Now she's hurt herself.

ANNIE [GRIMLY]: No, she hasn't.

KELLER: Will you please let her hands go?

KATE: Miss Annie, you don't know the child well
enough yet, she'll keep—

ANNIE: I know an ordinary tantrum well enough, when
I see one, and a badly spoiled child—

JAMES: Hear, hear.

KELLER [VERY ANNOYED]: Miss Sullivan! You would have
more understanding of your pupil if you had some
pity in you. Now kindly do as I—

ANNIE: Pity?

(*She releases* HELEN *to turn equally annoyed on*
KELLER *across the table; instantly* HELEN *scrambles
up and dives at* ANNIE'S *plate. This time* ANNIE *in-
tercepts her by pouncing on her wrists like a hawk,
and her temper boils.*)

For this *tyrant?* The whole house turns on her
whims, is there anything she wants she doesn't
get? I'll tell you what I pity, that the sun won't
rise and set for her all her life, and every day you're
telling her it will, what good will your pity do her
when you're under the strawberries, Captain Keller?

KELLER [OUTRAGED]: Kate, for the love of heaven will
you—

KATE: Miss Annie, please, I don't think it serves to lose our—

ANNIE: It does you good, that's all. It's less trouble to feel sorry for her than to teach her anything better, isn't it?

KELLER: I fail to see where you have taught her anything yet, Miss Sullivan!

ANNIE: I'll begin this minute, if you'll leave the room, Captain Keller!

KELLER [ASTONISHED]: Leave the—

ANNIE: Everyone, please.

(*She struggles with* HELEN, *while* KELLER *endeavors to control his voice.*)

KELLER: Miss Sullivan, you are here only as a paid teacher. Nothing more, and not to lecture—

ANNIE: I can't *un*teach her six years of pity if you can't stand up to one tantrum! Old Stonewall, indeed. Mrs. Keller, you promised me help.

KATE: Indeed I did, we truly want to—

ANNIE: Then leave me alone with her. Now!

KELLER [IN A WRATH]: Katie, will you come outside with me? At once, please.

(*He marches to the front door.* KATE *and* JAMES *follow him. Simultaneously* ANNIE *releases* HELEN's *wrists, and the child again sinks to the floor, kicking and crying her weird noises;* ANNIE *steps over her to meet* VINEY *coming in the rear doorway with biscuits and a clean plate, surprised at the general commotion.*)

224		*The Miracle Worker*

VINEY: Heaven sakes—
ANNIE: Out, please.

> (*She backs* VINEY *out with one hand, closes the door on her astonished mouth, locks it, and removes the key.* KELLER *meanwhile snatches his hat from a rack, and* KATE *follows him down the porch steps.* JAMES *lingers in the doorway to address* ANNIE *across the room with a bow.*)

JAMES: If it takes all summer, general.

> (ANNIE *comes over to his door in turn, removing her glasses grimly; as* KELLER *outside begins speaking,* ANNIE *closes the door on* JAMES, *locks it, removes the key, and turns with her back against the door to stare ominously at* HELEN, *kicking on the floor.*
>
> JAMES *takes his hat from the rack, and going down the porch steps joins* KATE *and* KELLER *talking in the yard,* KELLER *in a sputter of ire.*)

KELLER: This girl, this—cub of a girl—*presumes!* I tell you, I'm of half a mind to ship her back to Boston before the week is out. You can inform her so from me!
KATE [EYEBROWS UP]: I, Captain?
KELLER: She's a *hireling!* Now I want it clear, unless there's an apology and complete change of manner she goes back on the next train! Will you make that quite clear?

KATE: Where will you be, Captain, while I am making it quite—
KELLER: At the office!

(*He begins off left, finds his napkin still in his irate hand, is uncertain with it, dabs his lips with dignity, gets rid of it in a toss to* JAMES, *and marches off.* JAMES *turns to eye* KATE.)

JAMES: Will you?

(KATE's *mouth is set, and* JAMES *studies it lightly.*)

I thought what she said was exceptionally intelligent. I've been saying it for years.
KATE [NOT WITHOUT SCORN]: To his face?

(*She comes to relieve him of the white napkin, but reverts again with it.*)

Or will you take it, Jimmie? As a flag?

(JAMES *stalks out, much offended, and* KATE *turning stares across the yard at the house; the lights narrowing down to the following pantomime in the family room leave her motionless in the dark.*

ANNIE *meanwhile has begun by slapping both keys down on a shelf out of* HELEN's *reach; she returns to the table, upstage.* HELEN's *kicking has subsided, and when from the floor her hand finds* ANNIE's *chair empty she pauses.* ANNIE *clears the table of* KATE's, JAMES's, *and* KELLER's *plates; she gets back to her own across the table just in time to slide it*

deftly away from HELEN's *pouncing hand. She lifts
the hand and moves it to* HELEN's *plate, and after
an instant's exploration,* HELEN *sits again on the
floor and drums her heels.* ANNIE *comes around
the table and resumes her chair. When* HELEN *feels
her skirt again, she ceases kicking, waits for whatever is to come, renews some kicking, waits again.*
ANNIE *retrieving her plate takes up a forkful of
food, stops it halfway to her mouth, gazes at it
devoid of appetite, and half-lowers it; but after a
look at* HELEN *she sighs, dips the forkful toward*
HELEN *in a for-your-sake toast, and puts it in her
own mouth to chew, not without an effort.*

HELEN *now gets hold of the chair leg, and half-
succeeds in pulling the chair out from under her.*
ANNIE *bangs it down with her rear, heavily, and
sits with all her weight.* HELEN's *next attempt to
topple it is unavailing, so her fingers dive in a
pinch at* ANNIE's *flank.* ANNIE *in the middle of her
mouthful almost loses it with startle, and she slaps
down her fork to round on* HELEN. *The child comes
up with curiosity to feel what* ANNIE *is doing, so*
ANNIE *resumes eating, letting* HELEN's *hand follow
the movement of her fork to her mouth; whereupon* HELEN *at once reaches into* ANNIE's *plate.*
ANNIE *firmly removes her hand to her own plate.*
HELEN *in reply pinches* ANNIE's *thigh, a good mean
pinchful that makes* ANNIE *jump.* ANNIE *sets the
fork down, and sits with her mouth tight.* HELEN
digs another pinch into her thigh, and this time
ANNIE *slaps her hand smartly away;* HELEN *retali-
ates with a roundhouse fist that catches* ANNIE *on*

the ear, and ANNIE'S *hand leaps at once in a force-
ful slap across* HELEN'S *cheek;* HELEN *is the startled
one now.* ANNIE'S *hand in compunction falters to
her own face, but when* HELEN *hits at her again,*
ANNIE *deliberately slaps her again.* HELEN *lifts her
fist irresolute for another roundhouse,* ANNIE *lifts
her hand resolute for another slap, and they freeze
in this posture, while* HELEN *mulls it over. She thinks
better of it, drops her fist, and giving* ANNIE *a wide
berth, gropes around to her* MOTHER'S *chair, to find
it empty; she blunders her way along the table,
upstage, and encountering the empty chairs and
missing plates, she looks bewildered; she gropes
back to her* MOTHER'S *chair, again touches her
cheek and indicates the chair, and waits for the
world to answer.*

ANNIE *now reaches over to spell into her hand, but*
HELEN *yanks it away; she gropes to the front door,
tries the knob, and finds the door locked, with no
key. She gropes to the rear door, and finds it
locked, with no key. She commences to bang on it.*
ANNIE *rises, crosses, takes her wrists, draws her re-
sisting back to the table, seats her, and releases her
hands upon her plate; as* ANNIE *herself begins to sit,*
HELEN *writhes out of her chair, runs to the front
door, and tugs and kicks at it.* ANNIE *rises again,
crosses, draws her by one wrist back to the table,
seats her, and sits;* HELEN *escapes back to the door,
knocking over her* MOTHER'S *chair en route.* ANNIE
rises again in pursuit, and this time lifts HELEN
*bodily from behind and bears her kicking to her
chair. She deposits her, and once more turns to sit.*

HELEN *scrambles out, but as she passes* ANNIE *catches her up again from behind and deposits her in the chair;* HELEN *scrambles out on the other side, for the rear door, but* ANNIE *at her heels catches her up and deposits her again in the chair. She stands behind it.* HELEN *scrambles out to her right, and the instant her feet hit the floor* ANNIE *lifts and deposits her back; she scrambles out to her left, and is at once lifted and deposited back. She tries right again and is deposited back, and tries left again and is deposited back, and now feints* ANNIE *to the right but is off to her left, and is promptly deposited back. She sits a moment, and then starts straight over the tabletop, dishware notwithstanding;* ANNIE *hauls her in and deposits her back, with her plate spilling in her lap, and she melts to the floor and crawls under the table, laborious among its legs and chairs; but* ANNIE *is swift around the table and waiting on the other side when she surfaces, immediately bearing her aloft;* HELEN *clutches at* JAMES'S *chair for anchorage, but it comes with her, and halfway back she abandons it to the floor.* ANNIE *deposits her in her chair, and waits.* HELEN *sits tensed motionless. Then she tentatively puts out her left foot and hand,* ANNIE *interposes her own hand, and at the contact* HELEN *jerks hers in. She tries her right foot,* ANNIE *blocks it with her own, and* HELEN *jerks hers in. Finally, leaning back, she slumps down in her chair, in a sullen biding.*

ANNIE *backs off a step, and watches;* HELEN *offers no move.* ANNIE *takes a deep breath. Both of them and the room are in considerable disorder, two chairs down and the table a mess, but* ANNIE *makes no effort to tidy it; she only sits on her own chair, and lets her energy refill. Then she takes up knife and fork, and resolutely addresses her food.* HELEN'S *hand comes out to explore, and seeing it* ANNIE *sits without moving; the child's hand goes over her hand and fork, pauses—*ANNIE *still does not move—and withdraws. Presently it moves for her own plate, slaps about for it, and stops, thwarted. At this,* ANNIE *again rises, recovers* HELEN'S *plate from the floor and a handful of scattered food from the deranged tablecloth, drops it on the plate, and pushes the plate into contact with* HELEN'S *fist. Neither of them now moves for a pregnant moment—until* HELEN *suddenly takes a grab of food and wolfs it down.* ANNIE *permits herself the humor of a minor bow and warming of her hands together; she wanders off a step or two, watching.* HELEN *cleans up the plate.*

After a glower of indecision, she holds the empty plate out for more. ANNIE *accepts it, and crossing to the removed plates, spoons food from them onto it; she stands debating the spoon, tapping it a few times on* HELEN'S *plate; and when she returns with the plate she brings the spoon, too. She puts the spoon first into* HELEN'S *hand, then sets the plate down.* HELEN *discarding the spoon reaches with her hand, and* ANNIE *stops it by the wrist; she replaces the spoon in it.* HELEN *impatiently discards it again, and again* ANNIE *stops her hand, to replace the spoon in it. This time* HELEN *throws the spoon on the floor.* ANNIE *after considering it lifts* HELEN *bodily out of the chair, and in a wrestling match on the floor closes her fingers upon the spoon, and returns her with it to the chair.* HELEN *again throws the spoon on the floor.* ANNIE *lifts her out of the chair again; but in the struggle over the spoon* HELEN *with* ANNIE *on her back sends her sliding over her head;* HELEN *flees back to her chair and scrambles into it. When* ANNIE *comes after her she clutches it for dear life;* ANNIE *pries one hand loose, then the other, then the first again, then the other again, and then lifts* HELEN *by the waist, chair and all, and shakes the chair loose.* HELEN *wrestles to get free, but* ANNIE *pins her to the floor, closes her fingers upon the spoon, and lifts her kicking under one arm; with her other hand she gets the chair in place again, and plunks* HELEN *back on it. When she releases her hand,* HELEN *throws the spoon at her.*

ANNIE *now removes the plate of food.* HELEN *grabbing finds it missing, and commences to bang with her fists on the table.* ANNIE *collects a fistful of spoons and descends with them and the plate on* HELEN; *she lets her smell the plate, at which* HELEN *ceases banging, and* ANNIE *puts the plate down and a spoon in* HELEN's *hand.* HELEN *throws it on the floor.* ANNIE *puts another spoon in her hand.* HELEN *throws it on the floor.* ANNIE *puts another spoon in her hand.* HELEN *throws it on the floor. When* ANNIE *comes to her last spoon she sits next to* HELEN, *and gripping the spoon in* HELEN's *hand compels her to take food in it up to her mouth.*

HELEN *sits with lips shut.* ANNIE *waits a stolid mo-*
ment, then lowers HELEN's *hand. She tries again;*
HELEN's *lips remain shut.* ANNIE *waits, lowers*
HELEN's *hand. She tries again; this time* HELEN
suddenly opens her mouth and accepts the food.
ANNIE *lowers the spoon with a sigh of relief, and*
HELEN *spews the mouthful out at her face.* ANNIE
sits a moment with eyes closed, then takes the
pitcher and dashes its water into HELEN's *face, who*
gasps astonished. ANNIE *with* HELEN's *hand takes*
up another spoonful, and shoves it into her open
mouth. HELEN *swallows involuntarily, and while*
she is catching her breath ANNIE *forces her palm*
open, throws four swift letters into it, then another
four, and bows toward her with devastating pleas-
antness.)

ANNIE: Good girl.

(ANNIE *lifts* HELEN's *hand to feel her face nodding;*
HELEN *grabs a fistful of her hair, and yanks. The*
pain brings ANNIE *to her knees, and* HELEN *pum-*
mels her; they roll under the table, and the lights
commence to dim out on them.

Simultaneously the light at left has been rising,
slowly, so slowly that it seems at first we only imag-
ine what is intimated in the yard: a few ghostlike
figures, in silence, motionless, waiting. Now the
distant belfry chimes commence to toll the hour,
also very slowly, almost—it is twelve—intermina-
bly; the sense is that of a long time passing. We
can identify the figures before the twelfth stroke,

all facing the house in a kind of watch: KATE *is
standing exactly as before, but now with the baby
MILDRED sleeping in her arms, and placed here
and there, unmoving, are AUNT EV in her hat with
a hanky to her nose, and the two Negro children,
PERCY and MARTHA with necks outstretched ea-
gerly, and VINEY with a knotted kerchief on her
head and a feather duster in her hand.*

*The chimes cease, and there is silence. For a long
moment none of the group moves.)*

VINEY [PRESENTLY]: What am I gone do, Miss Kate?
It's noontime, dinner's comin', I didn't get them
breakfast dishes out of there yet.

(KATE *says nothing, stares at the house.* MARTHA
shifts HELEN's *doll in her clutch, and it plaintively
says momma.)*

KATE [PRESENTLY]: You run along, Martha.

(AUNT EV *blows her nose.)*

AUNT EV [WRETCHEDLY]: I can't wait out here a minute
longer, Kate, why, this could go on all afternoon,
too.
KATE: I'll tell the Captain you called.
VINEY [TO THE CHILDREN]: You hear what Miss Kate
say? Never you mind what's going on here.

(*Still no one moves.)*

You run along tend your own bizness.

(*Finally* viney *turns on the children with the feather duster.*)

Shoo!

(*The two children divide before her. She chases them off.* aunt ev *comes to* kate, *on her dignity.*)

aunt ev: Say what you like, Kate, but that child is a *Keller.*

(*She opens her parasol, preparatory to leaving.*)

I needn't remind you that all the Kellers are cousins to General Robert E. Lee. I don't know *who* that girl is.

(*She waits; but* kate *staring at the house is without response.*)

The only Sullivan I've heard of—from Boston too, and I'd think twice before locking her up with that kind—is that man John L.

(*And* aunt ev *departs, with head high. Presently* viney *comes to* kate, *her arms out for the baby.*)

viney: You give me her, Miss Kate, I'll sneak her in back, to her crib.

(*But* KATE *is moveless, until* VINEY *starts to take
the baby;* KATE *looks down at her before relin-
quishing her.*)

KATE [SLOWLY]: This child never gives me a minute's
worry.

VINEY: Oh yes, this one's the angel of the family, no
question bout *that*.

(*She begins off rear with the baby, heading around
the house; and* KATE *now turns her back on it, her
hand to her eyes. At this moment there is the
slamming of a door, and when* KATE *wheels* HELEN
*is blundering down the porch steps into the light,
like a ruined bat out of hell.* VINEY *halts, and* KATE
runs in; HELEN *collides with her mother's knees,
and reels off and back to clutch them as her savior.*
ANNIE *with smoked glasses in hand stands on the
porch, also much undone, looking as though she
had indeed just taken Vicksburg.* KATE *taking in*
HELEN's *ravaged state becomes steely in her gaze
up at* ANNIE.)

KATE: What happened?

(ANNIE *meets* KATE's *gaze, and gives a factual report, too exhausted for anything but a flat voice.*)

ANNIE: She ate from her own plate.

(*She thinks a moment.*)

She ate with a spoon. Herself.

(KATE *frowns, uncertain with thought, and glances down at* HELEN.)

And she folded her napkin.

(KATE'S *gaze now wavers, from* HELEN *to* ANNIE, *and back.*)

KATE [SOFTLY]: Folded—her napkin?
ANNIE: The room's a wreck, but her napkin is folded.

(*She pauses, then:*)

I'll be in my room, Mrs. Keller.

(*She moves to re-enter the house; but she stops at* VINEY'S *voice.*)

VINEY [CHEERY]: Don't be long, Miss Annie. Dinner be ready right away!

(VINEY *carries* MILDRED *around the back of the house.* ANNIE *stands unmoving, takes a deep breath, stares over her shoulder at* KATE *and* HELEN, *then inclines her head graciously, and goes with a slight stagger into the house. The lights in her room above steal up in readiness for her.*

KATE *remains alone with* HELEN *in the yard, standing protectively over her, in a kind of wonder.*)

KATE [SLOWLY]: Folded her napkin.

(She contemplates the wild head in her thighs, and moves her fingertips over it, with such a tenderness, and something like a fear of its strangeness, that her own eyes close; she whispers, bending to it:)

My Helen—folded her napkin—

(And still erect, with only her head in surrender, KATE for the first time that we see loses her protracted war with grief; but she will not let a sound escape her, only the grimace of tears comes, and sobs that shake her in a grip of silence. But HELEN feels them, and her hand comes up in its own wondering, to interrogate her mother's face, until KATE buries her lips in the child's palm.

Upstairs, ANNIE enters her room, closes the door, and stands back against it; the lights, growing on her with their special color, commence to fade on KATE and HELEN. Then ANNIE goes wearily to her suitcase, and lifts it to take it toward the bed. But it knocks an object to the floor, and she turns back to regard it. A new voice comes in a cultured murmur, hesitant as with the effort of remembering a text:)

MAN'S VOICE: This—soul—

(ANNIE puts the suitcase down, and kneels to the object: it is the battered Perkins report, and she stands with it in her hand, letting memory try to speak:)

This—blind, deaf, mute—woman—

(ANNIE *sits on her bed, opens the book, and finding the passage, brings it up an inch from her eyes
to read, her face and lips following the overheard
words, the voice quite factual now*:)

Can nothing be done to disinter this human soul?
The whole neighborhood would rush to save this
woman if she were buried alive by the caving in of
a pit, and labor with zeal until she were dug out.
Now if there were one who had as much patience
as zeal, he might awaken her to a consciousness
of her immortal—

(*When the boy's voice comes,* ANNIE *closes her
eyes, in pain.*)

BOY'S VOICE: Annie? Annie, you there?
ANNIE: Hush.
BOY'S VOICE: Annie, what's that noise?

(ANNIE *tries not to answer; her own voice is drawn
out of her, unwilling.*)

ANNIE: Just a cot, Jimmie.
BOY'S VOICE: Where they pushin' it?
ANNIE: To the deadhouse.
BOY'S VOICE: Annie. Does it hurt, to be dead?

(ANNIE *escapes by opening her eyes, her hand
works restlessly over her cheek; she retreats into
the book again, but the cracked old crones inter-
rupt, whispering.* ANNIE *slowly lowers the book.*)

FIRST CRONE'S VOICE: There is schools.

SECOND CRONE'S VOICE: There is schools outside—

THIRD CRONE'S VOICE: —schools where they teach blind
   ones, worse'n you—

FIRST CRONE'S VOICE: To read—

SECOND CRONE'S VOICE: To read and write—

THIRD CRONE'S VOICE: There is schools outside where
   they—

FIRST CRONE'S VOICE: There is schools—

(*Silence.* ANNIE *sits with her eyes shining, her hand
almost in a caress over the book. Then:*)

BOY'S VOICE: You ain't goin' to school, are you, Annie?

ANNIE [WHISPERING]: When I grow up.

BOY'S VOICE: You ain't either, Annie. You're goin' to
   stay here take care of me.

ANNIE: I'm goin' to school when I grow up.

BOY'S VOICE: You said we'll be together, forever and
   ever and ever—

ANNIE [FIERCE]: I'm goin' to school when I grow up!

DOCTOR'S VOICE [SLOWLY]: Little girl. Little girl, I must
   tell you. Your brother will be going on a journey,
   soon.

(ANNIE *sits rigid, in silence. Then the boy's voice
pierces it, a shriek of terror.*)

BOY'S VOICE: *Annie!*

(*It goes into* ANNIE *like a sword, she doubles onto
it; the book falls to the floor. It takes her a racked*

*moment to find herself and what she was engaged
in here; when she sees the suitcase she remembers,
and lifts it once again toward the bed. But the
voices are with her, as she halts with suitcase in
hand.)*

FIRST CRONE'S VOICE: Goodbye, Annie.

DOCTOR'S VOICE: Write me when you learn how.

SECOND CRONE'S VOICE: Don't tell anyone you came
from here. Don't tell anyone—

THIRD CRONE'S VOICE: Yeah, don't tell anyone you came
from—

FIRST CRONE'S VOICE: Yeah, don't tell anyone—

SECOND CRONE'S VOICE: Don't tell any—

(The echoing voices fade. After a moment ANNIE
*lays the suitcase on the bed; and the last voice
comes faintly, from far away.)*

BOY'S VOICE: Annie. It hurts, to be dead. Forever.

*(*ANNIE *falls to her knees by the bed, stifling her
mouth in it. When at last she rolls blindly away
from it, her palm comes down on the open report;
she opens her eyes, regards it dully, and then, still
on her knees, takes in the print.)*

MAN'S VOICE [FACTUAL]: —might awaken her to a consciousness of her immortal nature. The chance is
small indeed; but with a smaller chance they
would have dug desperately for her in the pit; and
is the life of the soul of less import than that of
the body?

(ANNIE *gets to her feet. She drops the book on the
bed, and pauses over her suitcase; after a moment
she unclasps and opens it. Standing before it, she
comes to her decision; she at once turns to the
bureau, and taking her things out of its drawers,
commences to throw them into the open suitcase.*

*In the darkness down left a hand strikes a match,
and lights a hanging oil lamp. It is* KELLER's *hand,
and his voice accompanies it, very angry; the lights
rising here before they fade on* ANNIE *show* KELLER
and KATE *inside a suggestion of a garden house,
with a bay-window seat towards center and a door
at back.*)

KELLER: Katie, I will not *have* it! Now you did not see
when that girl after supper tonight went to look
for Helen in her room—

KATE: No.

KELLER: The child practically climbed out of her window to escape from her! What kind of teacher *is*
she? I thought I had seen her at her worst this
morning, shouting at me, but I come home to
find the entire house disorganized by her—Helen
won't stay one second in the same room, won't
come to the table with her, won't let herself be
bathed or undressed or put to bed by her, or even
by Viney now, and the end result is that *you* have
to do more for the child than before we hired this
girl's services! From the moment she stepped off
the train she's been nothing but a burden, incom-
petent, impertinent, ineffectual, immodest—

KATE: She folded her napkin, Captain.

KELLER: What?

KATE: Not ineffectual. Helen did fold her napkin.

KELLER: What is heaven's name is so extraordinary about folding a napkin?

KATE [WITH SOME HUMOR]: Well. It's more than you did, Captain.

KELLER: Katie. I did not bring you all the way out here to the garden house to be frivolous. Now, how does Miss Sullivan propose to teach a deaf-blind pupil who won't let her even touch her?

KATE [A PAUSE]: I don't know.

KELLER: The fact is, today she scuttled any chance she ever had of getting along with the child. If you can see any point or purpose to her staying on here longer, it's more than—

KATE: What do you wish me to do?

KELLER: I want you to give her notice.

KATE: I can't.

KELLER: Then if you won't, I must. I simply will not—

(*He is interrupted by a knock at the back door.* KELLER *after a glance at* KATE *moves to open the door;* ANNIE *in her smoked glasses is standing outside.* KELLER *contemplates her, heavily.*)

Miss Sullivan.

ANNIE: Captain Keller.

(*She is nervous, keyed up to seizing the bull by the horns again, and she assumes a cheeriness which is not unshaky.*)

Viney said I'd find you both over here in the garden house. I thought we should—have a talk?

KELLER [RELUCTANTLY]: Yes, I— Well, come in.

(ANNIE *enters, and is interested in this room; she
rounds on her heel, anxiously, studying it.* KELLER
turns the matter over to KATE, *sotto voce.*)

Katie.

KATE [TURNING IT BACK, COURTEOUSLY]: Captain.

(KELLER *clears his throat, makes ready.*)

KELLER: I, ah—wanted first to make my position clear
to Mrs. Keller, in private. I have decided I—am
not satisfied—in fact, am deeply dissatisfied—with
the manner in which—

ANNIE [INTENT]: Excuse me, is this little house ever in
use?

KELLER [WITH PATIENCE]: In the hunting season. If you
will give me your attention, Miss Sullivan.

(ANNIE *turns her smoked glasses upon him; they
hold his unwilling stare.*)

I have tried to make allowances for you because
you come from a part of the country where people
are—women, I should say—come from who—well,
for whom—

(*It begins to elude him.*)

—allowances must—be made. I have decided, nevertheless, to—that is, decided I—

(*Vexedly*)

Miss Sullivan, I find it difficult to talk through those glasses.

ANNIE [EAGERLY, REMOVING THEM]: Oh, of course.

KELLER [DOURLY]: Why do you wear them, the sun has been down for an hour.

ANNIE [PLEASANTLY, AT THE LAMP]: Any kind of light hurts my eyes.

(A *silence*; KELLER *ponders her, heavily.*)

KELLER: Put them on. Miss Sullivan, I have decided to—give you another chance.

ANNIE [CHEERFULLY]: To do what?

KELLER: To—remain in our employ.

(ANNIE'S *eyes widen.*)

But on two conditions. I am not accustomed to rudeness in servants or women, and that is the first. If you are to stay, there must be a radical change of manner.

ANNIE [A PAUSE]: Whose?

KELLER [EXPLODING]: Yours, young lady, isn't it obvious? And the second is that you persuade me there's the slightest hope of your teaching a child who flees from you now like the plague, to anyone else she can find in this house.

ANNIE [A PAUSE]: There isn't.

(KATE *stops sewing, and fixes her eyes upon* ANNIE.)

KATE: What, Miss Annie?

ANNIE: It's hopeless here. I can't teach a child who runs away.

KELLER [NONPLUSSED]: Then—do I understand you—propose—

ANNIE: Well, if we all agree it's hopeless, the next question is what—

KATE: Miss Annie.

(*She is leaning toward* ANNIE, *in deadly earnest; it commands both* ANNIE *and* KELLER.)

I am not agreed. I think perhaps you—underestimate Helen.

ANNIE: I think everybody else here does.

KATE: She did fold her napkin. She learns, she learns, do you know she began talking when she was six months old? She could say "water." Not really—"wahwah." "Wahwah," but she meant water, she knew what it meant, and only six months old, I never saw a child so—bright, or outgoing—

(*Her voice is unsteady, but she gets it level.*)

It's still in her, somewhere, isn't it? You should have seen her before her illness, such a good-tempered child—

ANNIE [AGREEABLY]: She's changed.

(*A pause,* KATE *not letting her eyes go; her appeal at last is unconditional, and very quiet.*)

KATE: Miss Annie, put up with it. And with us.

KELLER: Us!

KATE: Please? Like the lost lamb in the parable, I love her all the more.

ANNIE: Mrs. Keller, I don't think Helen's worst handicap is deafness or blindness. I think it's your love. And pity.

KELLER: Now what does that mean?

ANNIE: All of you here are so sorry for her you've kept her—like a pet, why, even a dog you housebreak. No wonder she won't let me come near her. It's useless for me to try to teach her language or anything else here. I might as well—

KATE [CUTS IN]: Miss Annie, before you came we spoke of putting her in an asylum.

(ANNIE *turns back to regard her. A pause.*)

ANNIE: What kind of asylum?

KELLER: For mental defectives.

KATE: I visited there. I can't tell you what I saw, people like—animals, with—*rats*, in the halls, and—

(*She shakes her head on her vision.*)

What else are we to do, if you give up?

ANNIE: Give up?

KATE: You said it was hopeless.

ANNIE: Here. Give up, why, I only today saw what has to be done, to begin!

(*She glances from* KATE *to* KELLER, *who stare, waiting; and she makes it as plain and simple as her nervousness permits.*)

I—want complete charge of her.

KELLER: You already have that. It has resulted in—

ANNIE: No, I mean day and night. She has to be dependent on me.

KATE: For what?

ANNIE: Everything. The food she eats, the clothes she wears, fresh—

(*She is amused at herself, though very serious.*)

—air, yes, the air she breathes, whatever her body needs is a—primer, to teach her out of. It's the only way, the one who lets her have it should be her teacher.

(*She considers them in turn; they digest it,* KELLER *frowning,* KATE *perplexed.*)

Not anyone who *loves* her, you have so many feelings they fall over each other like feet, you won't use your chances and you won't let me.

KATE: But if she runs from you—*to* us—

ANNIE: Yes, that's the point. I'll have to live with her somewhere else.

KELLER: What!

ANNIE: Till she learns to depend on and listen to me.

KATE [NOT WITHOUT ALARM]: For how long?

ANNIE: As long as it takes.

(*A pause. She takes a breath.*)

I packed half my things already.

KELLER: Miss—Sullivan!

(*But when* ANNIE *attends upon him he is speech-less, and she is merely earnest.*)

ANNIE: Captain Keller, it meets both your conditions. It's the one way I can get back in touch with Helen, and I don't see how I can be rude to you again if you're not around to interfere with me.

KELLER [RED-FACED]: And what is your intention if I say no? Pack the other half, for home, and abandon your charge to—to—

ANNIE: The asylum?

(*She waits, appraises* KELLER's *glare and* KATE's *uncertainty, and decides to use her weapons.*)

I grew up in such an asylum. The state almshouse.

(KATE's *head comes up on this, and* KELLER *stares hard;* ANNIE's *tone is cheerful enough, albeit level as gunfire.*)

Rats—why, my brother Jimmie and I used to play with the rats because we didn't have toys. Maybe you'd like to know what Helen will find there, not on visiting days? One ward was full of the—old women, crippled, blind, most of them dying, but even if what they had was catching there was nowhere else to move them, and that's where they put us. There were younger ones across the hall, prostitutes mostly, with T.B., and epileptic fits, and a couple of the kind who—keep after other

girls, especially young ones, and some insane. Some
just had the D.T.'s. The youngest were in another
ward to have babies they didn't want, they started
at thirteen, fourteen. They'd leave afterwards, but
the babies stayed and we played with them, too,
though a lot of them had—sores all over from dis-
eases you're not supposed to talk about, but not
many of them lived. The first year we had eighty,
seventy died. The room Jimmie and I played in
was the deadhouse, where they kept the bodies till
they could dig—

KATE [CLOSES HER EYES]: Oh, my dear—

ANNIE: —the graves.

(*She is immune to* KATE'S *compassion.*)

No, it made me strong. But I don't think you need
send Helen there. She's strong enough.

(*She waits again; but when neither offers her a
a word, she simply concludes.*)

No, I have no conditions, Captain Keller.

KATE [NOT LOOKING UP]: Miss Annie.

ANNIE: Yes.

KATE [A PAUSE]: Where would you—take Helen?

ANNIE: Ohh—

(*Brightly*)

Italy?

KELLER [WHEELING]: What?

ANNIE: Can't have everything, how would this garden
house do? Furnish it, bring Helen here after a long
ride so she won't recognize it, and you can see her
every day. If she doesn't know. Well?

KATE [A SIGH OF RELIEF]: Is that all?

ANNIE: That's all.

KATE: Captain.

(KELLER *turns his head; and* KATE's *request is quiet
but firm.*)

With your permission?

KELLER [TEETH IN CIGAR]: Why must she depend on
you for the food she eats?

ANNIE [A PAUSE]: I want control of it.

KELLER: Why?

ANNIE: It's a way to reach her.

KELLER [STARES]: You intend to *starve* her into letting
you touch her?

ANNIE: She won't starve, she'll learn. All's fair in love
and war, Captain Keller, you never cut supplies?

KELLER: This is hardly a war!

ANNIE: Well, it's not love. A siege is a siege.

KELLER [HEAVILY]: Miss Sullivan. Do you *like* the child?

ANNIE [STRAIGHT IN HIS EYES]: Do you?

(A *long pause.*)

KATE: You could have a servant here—

ANNIE [AMUSED]: I'll have enough work without looking after a servant! But that boy Percy could sleep
here, run errands—

KATE [ALSO AMUSED]: We can let Percy sleep here, I
    think, Captain?

ANNIE [EAGERLY]: And some old furniture, all our
    own—

KATE [ALSO EAGER]: Captain? Do you think that walnut
    bedstead in the barn would be too—

KELLER: I have not yet consented to Percy! Or to the
    house, or to the proposal! Or to Miss Sullivan's—
    staying on when I—

(*But he erupts in an irate surrender.*)

Very well, I consent to everything!

(*He shakes the cigar at* ANNIE.)

For two weeks. I'll give you two weeks in this
place, and it will be a miracle if you get the child
to tolerate you.

KATE: Two weeks? Miss Annie, can you accomplish
    anything in two weeks?

KELLER: Anything or not, two weeks, then the child
    comes back to us. Make up your mind, Miss Sulli-
    van, yes or no?

ANNIE: Two weeks. For only one miracle?

(*She nods at him, nervously.*)

I'll get her to tolerate me.

(KELLER *marches out, and slams the door.* KATE *on
her feet regards* ANNIE, *who is facing the door.*)

KATE [THEN]: You can't think as little of love as you said.

(ANNIE *glances questioning.*)

Or you wouldn't stay.

ANNIE [A PAUSE]: I didn't come here for love. I came for money!

(KATE *shakes her head to this, with a smile; after a moment she extends her open hand.* ANNIE *looks at it, but when she puts hers out it is not to shake hands, it is to set her fist in* KATE's *palm.*)

KATE [PUZZLED]: Hm?

ANNIE: A. It's the first of many. Twenty-six!

(KATE *squeezes her fist, squeezes it hard, and hastens out after* KELLER. ANNIE *stands as the door closes behind her, her manner so apprehensive that finally she slaps her brow, holds it, sighs, and, with her eyes closed, crosses herself for luck.*

The lights dim into a cool silhouette scene around her, the lamp paling out, and now, in formal entrances, persons appear around ANNIE *with furniture for the room:* PERCY *crosses the stage with a rocking chair and waits;* MARTHA *from another direction bears in a stool,* VINEY *bears in a small table, and the other Negro servant rolls in a bed partway from left; and* ANNIE, *opening her eyes to put her glasses back on, sees them. She turns around in the room once, and goes into action,*

place them and leave, and ANNIE then darts around,
interchanging them. In the midst of this—while
PERCY and MARTHA reappear with a tray of food
and a chair, respectively—JAMES comes down from
the house with ANNIE's suitcase, and stands view-
ing the room and her quizzically; ANNIE halts
abruptly under his eye, embarrassed, then seizes
the suitcase from his hand, explaining herself
brightly.)*

ANNIE: I always wanted to live in a doll's house!

*(She sets the suitcase out of the way, and contin-
ues; VINEY at left appears to position a rod with
drapes for a doorway, and the other servant at center pushes in a wheelbarrow loaded with a couple
of boxes of HELEN's toys and clothes. ANNIE helps
lift them into the room, and the servant pushes
the wheelbarrow off. In none of this is any heed
taken of the imaginary walls of the garden house,
the furniture is moved in from every side and itself
defines the walls.*

*ANNIE now drags the box of toys into center, props
up the doll conspicuously on top; with the people
melted away, except for JAMES, all is again still.
The lights turn again without pause, rising
warmer.)*

JAMES: You don't let go of things easily, do you? How
will you—win her hand now, in this place?

ANNIE [CURTLY]: Do I know? I lost my temper, and
here we are!

JAMES [LIGHTLY]: No touching, no teaching. Of course,
you *are* bigger—

ANNIE: I'm not counting on force, I'm counting on her.
That little imp is dying to know.

JAMES: Know what?

ANNIE: Anything. Any and every crumb in God's creation. I'll have to use that appetite too.

(*She gives the room a final survey, straightens the
bed, arranges the curtains.*)

JAMES [A PAUSE]: Maybe she'll teach you.

ANNIE: Of course.

JAMES: That she isn't. That there's such a thing as—
dullness of heart. Acceptance. And letting go.
Sooner or later we all give up, don't we?

ANNIE: Maybe you all do. It's my idea of the original
sin.

JAMES: What is?

ANNIE [WITHERINGLY]: Giving up.

JAMES [NETTLED]: You won't open her. Why can't you
let her be? Have some—pity on her, for being what
she is—

ANNIE: If I'd ever once thought like that, I'd be dead!

JAMES [PLEASANTLY]: You will be. Why trouble?

(ANNIE *turns to glare at him; he is mocking.*)

Or will you teach me?

(*And with a bow, he drifts off.*

Now in the distance there comes the clopping of hoofs, drawing near, and nearer, up to the door; and they halt. ANNIE *wheels to face the door. When it opens this time, the* KELLERS—KATE *in travelling bonnet,* KELLER *also hatted—are standing there with* HELEN *between them; she is in a cloak.* KATE *gently cues her into the room.* HELEN *comes in groping, baffled, but interested in the new surroundings;* ANNIE *evades her exploring hand, her gaze not leaving the child.*)

ANNIE: Does she know where she is?

KATE [SHAKES HER HEAD]: We rode her out in the country for two hours.

KELLER: For all she knows, she could be in another town—

(HELEN *stumbles over the box on the floor and in it discovers her doll and other battered toys, is pleased, sits to them, then becomes puzzled and suddenly very wary. She scrambles up and back to her mother's thighs, but* ANNIE *steps in, and it is hers that* HELEN *embraces.* HELEN *recoils, gropes, and touches her cheek instantly.*)

KATE: That's her sign for me.

ANNIE: I know.

(HELEN *waits, then recommences her groping, more urgently.* KATE *stands indecisive, and takes an abrupt step toward her, but* ANNIE'S *hand is a barrier.*)

In two weeks.

KATE: Miss Annie, I— Please be good to her. These two weeks, try to be very good to her—

ANNIE: I will.

(KATE, *turning then, hurries out. The* KELLERS *cross back of the main house.*

ANNIE *closes the door.* HELEN *starts at the door jar, and rushes it.* ANNIE *holds her off.* HELEN *kicks her, breaks free, and careens around the room like an imprisoned bird, colliding with furniture, groping wildly, repeatedly touching her cheek in a growing panic. When she has covered the room, she commences her weird screaming.* ANNIE *moves to comfort her, but her touch sends* HELEN *into a paroxysm of rage: she tears away, falls over her box of toys, flings its contents in handfuls in* ANNIE's *direction, flings the box too, reels to her feet, rips curtains from the window, bangs and kicks at the door, sweeps objects off the mantelpiece and shelf, a little tornado incarnate, all destruction, until she comes upon her doll and, in the act of hurling it, freezes. Then she clutches it to herself, and in exhaustion sinks sobbing to the floor.* ANNIE *stands contemplating her, in some awe.*)

Two weeks.

(*She shakes her head, not without a touch of disgusted bewilderment.*)

What did I get into now?

(*The lights have been dimming throughout, and the garden house is lit only by moonlight now, with* ANNIE *lost in the patches of dark.*

KATE, *now hatless and coatless, enters the family room by the rear door, carrying a lamp.* KELLER, *also hatless, wanders simultaneously around the back of the main house to where* JAMES *has been waiting, in the rising moonlight, on the porch.*)

KELLER: I can't understand it. I had every intention of dismissing that girl, not setting her up like an empress.

JAMES: Yes, what's her secret, sir?

KELLER: Secret?

JAMES [PLEASANTLY]: That enables her to get anything she wants out of you? When I can't.

(JAMES *turns to go into the house, but* KELLER *grasps his wrist, twisting him half to his knees.* KATE *comes from the porch.*)

KELLER [ANGRILY]: She does *not* get anything she—

JAMES [IN PAIN]: Don't—don't—

KATE: Captain.

KELLER: He's afraid.

(*He throws* JAMES *away from him, with contempt.*)

What *does* he want out of me?

JAMES [AN OUTCRY]: My God, don't you know?

(*He gazes from* KELLER *to* KATE.)

Everything you forgot, when you forgot my
mother.

KELLER: What!

(JAMES *wheels into the house.* KELLER *takes a
stride to the porch, to roar after him.*)

One thing that girl's secret is not, she doesn't fire
one shot and disappear!

(KATE *stands rigid, and* KELLER *comes back to her.*)

Katie. Don't mind what he—

KATE: Captain, I am proud of you.

KELLER: For what?

KATE: For letting this girl have what she needs.

KELLER: Why can't my son be? He can't bear me,
you'd think I treat him as hard as this girl does
Helen—

(*He breaks off, as it dawns in him.*)

KATE [GENTLY]: Perhaps you do.

KELLER: But he has to learn some respect!

KATE [A PAUSE, WRYLY]: Do you like the child?

(*She turns again to the porch, but pauses, re-
luctant.*)

How empty the house is, tonight.

(*After a moment she continues on in.* KELLER
stands moveless, as the moonlight dies on him.

The distant belfry chimes toll, two o'clock, and with them, a moment later, comes the boy's voice on the wind, in a whisper:)

BOY'S VOICE: Annie. Annie.

(In her patch of dark ANNIE, *now in her night-gown, hurls a cup into a corner as though it were her grief, getting rid of its taste through her teeth.)*

ANNIE: No! No pity, I won't have it.

(She comes to HELEN, *prone on the floor.)*

On either of us.

(She goes to her knees, but when she touches HEL-EN's *hand the child starts up awake, recoils, and scrambles away from her under the bed.* ANNIE *stares after her. She strikes her palm on the floor, with passion.)*

I *will* touch you!

(She gets to her feet, and paces in a kind of anger around the bed, her hand in her hair, and con-fronting HELEN *at each turn.)*

How, how? How do I—

(ANNIE stops. Then she calls out urgently, loudly.)

Percy! Percy!

(*She moves swiftly to the drapes, at left.*)

Percy, wake up!

(PERCY'S *voice comes in a thick sleepy mumble, unintelligible.*)

Get out of bed and come in here, I need you.

(ANNIE *darts away, finds and strikes a match, and touches it to the hanging lamp; the lights come up dimly in the room, and* PERCY *stands bare to the waist in torn overalls between the drapes, with eyes closed, swaying.* ANNIE *goes to him, pats his cheeks vigorously.*)

Percy. You awake?
PERCY: No'm.
ANNIE: How would you like to play a nice game?
PERCY: Whah?
ANNIE: With Helen. She's under the bed. Touch her hand.

(*She kneels* PERCY *down at the bed, thrusting his hand under it to contact* HELEN'S; HELEN *emits an animal sound and crawls to the opposite side, but commences sniffing.* ANNIE *rounds the bed with* PERCY *and thrusts his hand again at* HELEN; *this time* HELEN *clutches it, sniffs in recognition, and comes scrambling out after* PERCY, *to hug him with delight.* PERCY *alarmed struggles, and* HELEN'S *fingers go to his mouth.*)

PERCY: Lemme go. Lemme go—

(HELEN *fingers her own lips, as before, moving them in dumb imitation.*)

She tryin' talk. She gonna hit me—
ANNIE [GRIMLY]: She *can* talk. If she only knew, I'll show you how. She makes letters.

(*She opens* PERCY'S *other hand, and spells into it:*)

This one is C. C.

(*She hits his palm with it a couple of times, her eyes upon* HELEN *across him;* HELEN *gropes to feel what* PERCY'S *hand is doing, and when she encounters* ANNIE'S *she falls back from them.*)

She's mad at me now, though, she won't play. But she knows lots of letters. Here's another, A. C, a. C, a.

(*But she is watching* HELEN, *who comes groping, consumed with curiosity;* ANNIE *makes the letters in* PERCY'S *hand, and* HELEN *pokes to question what they are up to. Then* HELEN *snatches* PERCY'S *other hand, and quickly spells four letters into it.* ANNIE *follows them aloud.*)

C, a, k, e! She spells cake, she gets cake.

(She is swiftly over to the tray of food, to fetch cake and a jug of milk.)

She doesn't know yet it means this. Isn't it funny she knows how to spell it and doesn't *know* she knows?

(She breaks the cake in two pieces, and extends one to each; HELEN rolls away from her offer.)

Well, if she won't play it with me, I'll play it with you. Would you like to learn one she doesn't know?

PERCY: No'm.

(But ANNIE seizes his wrist, and spells to him.)

ANNIE: M, i, l, k. M is this. I, that's an easy one, just the little finger. L is this—

(And HELEN comes back with her hand, to feel the new word. ANNIE brushes her away, and continues spelling aloud to PERCY. HELEN's hand comes back again, and tries to get in; ANNIE brushes it away again. HELEN's hand insists, and ANNIE puts it away rudely.)

No, why should I talk to you? I'm teaching Percy a new word. L. K is this—

(HELEN now yanks their hands apart; she butts PERCY away, and thrusts her palm out insistently. ANNIE's eyes are bright, with glee.)

Ho, you're *jealous*, are you!

(HELEN's *hand waits, intractably waits.*)

All *right.*

(ANNIE *spells into it, milk; and* HELEN *after a moment spells it back to* ANNIE. ANNIE *takes her hand, with her whole face shining. She gives a great sigh.*)

Good! So I'm finally back to where I can touch you, hm? Touch and go! No love lost, but here we go.

(*She puts the jug of milk into* HELEN's *hand and squeezes* PERCY's *shoulder.*)

You can go to bed now, you've earned your sleep. Thank you.

(PERCY *stumbling up weaves his way out through the drapes.* HELEN *finishes drinking, and holds the jug out, for* ANNIE; *when* ANNIE *takes it,* HELEN *crawls onto the bed, and makes for sleep.* ANNIE *stands, looks down at her.*)

Now all I have to teach you is—one word. Everything.

(*She sets the jug down. On the floor now* ANNIE *spies the doll, stoops to pick it up, and with it dangling in her hand, turns off the lamp. A shaft of moonlight is left on* HELEN *in the bed, and a second shaft on the rocking chair; and* ANNIE, *after putting off her smoked glasses, sits in the rocker with the doll. She is rather happy, and dangles the doll on her knee, and it makes its momma sound.* ANNIE *whispers to it in mock solicitude.*)

Hush, little baby. Don't—say a word—

(*She lays it against her shoulder, and begins rocking with it, patting its diminutive behind; she talks the lullaby to it, humorously at first.*)

  Momma's gonna buy you—a mockingbird:
  If that—mockingbird don't sing—

(*The rhythm of the rocking takes her into the tune, softly, and more tenderly.*)

  Momma's gonna buy you a diamond ring:
  If that diamond ring turns to brass—

(*A third shaft of moonlight outside now rises to pick out* JAMES *at the main house, with one foot on the porch step; he turns his body, as if hearing the song.*)

  Momma's gonna buy you a looking-glass:
  If that looking-glass gets broke—

(*In the family room a fourth shaft picks out* KELLER, *seated at the table, in thought; and he, too, lifts his head, as if hearing.*)

Momma's gonna buy you a billy goat:
If that billy goat won't pull—

(*The fifth shaft is upstairs in* ANNIE'S *room, and
picks out* KATE, *pacing there; and she halts, turning
her head, too, as if hearing.*)

Momma's gonna buy you a cart and bull:
If that cart and bull turns over,
Momma's gonna buy you a dog named Rover;
If that dog named Rover won't bark—

(*With the shafts of moonlight on* HELEN, *and*
JAMES, *and* KELLER, *and* KATE, *all moveless, and*
ANNIE *rocking the doll, the curtain ends the act.*)

ACT III

The stage is totally dark, until we see ANNIE *and* HELEN
silhouetted on the bed in the garden house. ANNIE'S
*voice is audible, very patient, and worn; it has been
saying this for a long time.*

ANNIE: Water, Helen. This is water. W, a, t, e, r. It
has a *name*.

(*A silence. Then:*)

Egg, e, g, g. It has a *name*, the name stands for
the thing. Oh, it's so simple, simple as birth, to
explain.

(*The lights have commenced to rise, not on the
garden house but on the homestead. Then:*)

Helen, Helen, the chick *has* to come out of its
shell, sometime. You come out, too.

(*In the bedroom upstairs, we see* VINEY *unhur-
riedly washing the window, dusting, turning the
mattress, readying the room for use again; then in
the family room a diminished group at one end of
the table—*KATE, KELLER, JAMES—*finishing up a
quiet breakfast; then outside, down right, the other
Negro servant on his knees, assisted by* MARTHA,
working with a trowel around a new trellis and

*wheelbarrow. The scene is one of everyday calm,
and all are oblivious to* ANNIE'S *voice.*)

There's only one way out, for you, and it's language. To learn that your fingers can talk. And say
anything, anything you can name. This is mug.
Mug, m, u, g. Helen, it has a *name*. It—has—a
—*name*—

(KATE *rises from the table.*)

KELLER [GENTLY]: You haven't eaten, Katie.

KATE [SMILES, SHAKES HER HEAD]: I haven't the appetite.
I'm too—restless, I can't sit to it.

KELLER: You should eat, my dear. It will be a long day,
waiting.

JAMES [LIGHTLY]: But it's been a short two weeks. I
never thought life could be so—noiseless, went
much too quickly for me.

(KATE *and* KELLER *gaze at him, in silence.* JAMES
becomes uncomfortable.)

ANNIE: C, a, r, d. Card. C, a—

JAMES: Well, the house has been practically normal,
hasn't it?

KELLER [HARSHLY]: Jimmie.

JAMES: Is it wrong to enjoy a quiet breakfast, after five
years? And you two even seem to enjoy each
other—

KELLER: It could be even more noiseless, Jimmie, without your tongue running every minute. Haven't

you enough feeling to imagine what Katie has been
undergoing, ever since—

(KATE *stops him, with her hand on his arm.*)

KATE: Captain.

(*To* JAMES.)

It's true. The two weeks have been normal, quiet,
all you say. But not short. Interminable.

(*She rises, and wanders out; she pauses on the
porch steps, gazing toward the garden house.*)

ANNIE [FADING]: W, a, t, e, r. But it means *this*.
W, a, t, e, r. *This*. W, a, t—
JAMES: I only meant that Miss Sullivan is a boon. Of
contention, though, it seems.
KELLER [HEAVILY]: If and when you're a parent, Jimmie,
you will understand what separation means. A
mother loses a—protector.
JAMES [BAFFLED]: Hm?
KELLER: You'll learn, we don't just keep our children
safe. They keep us safe.

(*He rises, with his empty coffee cup and saucer.*)

There are of course all kinds of separation, Katie
has lived with one kind for five years. And another
is disappointment. In a child.

(*He goes with the cup out the rear door.* JAMES
sits for a long moment of stillness. In the garden

house the lights commence to come up; ANNIE, *haggard at the table, is writing a letter, her face again almost in contact with the stationery;* HELEN, *apart on the stool, and for the first time as clean and neat as a button, is quietly crocheting an endless chain of wool, which snakes all around the room.)*

ANNIE: "I, feel, every, day, more, and, more, in—"

(She pauses, and turns the pages of a dictionary open before her; her finger descends the words to a full stop. She elevates her eyebrows, then copies the word.)

"—adequate."

(In the main house JAMES *pushes up, and goes to the front doorway, after* KATE.)*

JAMES: Kate?

*(*KATE *turns her glance.* JAMES *is rather weary.)*

I'm sorry. Open my mouth, like that fairy tale, frogs jump out.
KATE: No. It has been better. For everyone.

(She starts away, up center.)

ANNIE [WRITING]: "If, only, there, were, someone, to, help, me, I, need, a, teacher, as, much, as, Helen—"
JAMES: Kate.

*(*KATE *halts, waits.)*

What does he want from me?

KATE: That's not the question. Stand up to the world, Jimmie, that comes first.

JAMES [A PAUSE, WRYLY]: But the world is him.

KATE: Yes. And no one can do it for you.

JAMES: Kate.

(*His voice is humble.*)

At least we— Could you—be my friend?

KATE: I am.

(KATE *turns to wander, up back of the garden house.* ANNIE'S *murmur comes at once; the lights begin to die on the main house.*)

ANNIE: "—my, mind, is, undisiplined, full, of, skips, and, jumps, and—"

(*She halts, rereads, frowns.*)

Hm.

(ANNIE *puts her nose again in the dictionary, flips back to an earlier page, and fingers down the words;* KATE *presently comes down toward the bay window with a trayful of food.*)

Disinter—disinterested—disjoin—dis—

(*She backtracks, indignant.*)

Disinterested, disjoin— Where's disipline?

(She goes a page or two back, searching with her finger, muttering.)

What a dictionary, have to know how to spell it before you can look up how to spell it, disciple, *discipline!* Diskipline.

(She corrects the word in her letter.)

Undisciplined.

(But her eyes are bothering her, she closes them in exhaustion and gently fingers the eyelids. KATE *watches her through the window.)*

KATE: What are you doing to your eyes?

*(*ANNIE *glances around; she puts her smoked glasses on, and gets up to come over, assuming a cheerful energy.)*

ANNIE: It's worse on my vanity! I'm learning to spell. It's like a surprise party, the most unexpected characters turn up.
KATE: You're not to overwork your eyes, Miss Annie.
ANNIE: Well.

(She takes the tray, sets it on her chair, and carries chair and tray to HELEN.)*

Whatever I spell to Helen I'd better spell right.
KATE [ALMOST WISTFUL]: How—serene she is.

ANNIE: She learned this stitch yesterday. Now I can't get her to stop!

(*She disentangles one foot from the wool chain, and sets the chair before* HELEN. HELEN *at its contact with her knee feels the plate, promptly sets her crocheting down, and tucks the napkin in at her neck, but* ANNIE *withholds the spoon; when* HELEN *finds it missing, she folds her hands in her lap, and quietly waits.* ANNIE *twinkles at* KATE *with mock devoutness.*)

Such a little lady, she'd sooner starve than eat with her fingers.

(*She gives* HELEN *the spoon, and* HELEN *begins to eat, neatly.*)

KATE: You've taught her so much, these two weeks. I would never have—
ANNIE: Not enough.

(*She is suddenly gloomy, shakes her head.*)

Obedience isn't enough. Well, she learned two nouns this morning, key and water, brings her up to eighteen nouns and three verbs.
KATE [HESITANT]: But—not—
ANNIE: No. Not that they mean things. It's still a finger-game, no meaning.

(*She turns to* KATE, *abruptly.*)

Mrs. Keller—

(*But she defers it; she comes back, to sit in the bay
and lift her hand.*)

Shall we play our finger-game?
KATE: How will she learn it?
ANNIE: It will come.

(*She spells a word;* KATE *does not respond.*)

KATE: How?
ANNIE [A PAUSE]: How does a bird learn to fly?

(*She spells again.*)

We're born to use words, like wings, it has to come.
KATE: How?
ANNIE [ANOTHER PAUSE, WEARILY]: All right. I don't
know how.

(*She pushes up her glasses, to rub her eyes.*)

I've done everything I could think of. Whatever
she's learned here—keeping herself clean, knitting,
stringing beads, meals, setting-up exercises each
morning, we climb trees, hunt eggs, yesterday a
chick was born in her hands—all of it I spell,
everything we do, we never stop spelling. I go to
bed with—writer's cramp from talking so much!
KATE: I worry about you, Miss Annie. You must rest.
ANNIE: Now? She spells back in her *sleep*, her fingers
make letters when she doesn't know! In her bones

those five fingers know, that hand aches to—speak
out, and something in her mind is asleep, how do
I—nudge that awake? That's the one question.

KATE: With no answer.

ANNIE [LONG PAUSE]: Except keep at it. Like this.

(*She again begins spelling—I, need—and* KATE's
brows gather, following the words.)

KATE: More—time?

(*She glances at* ANNIE, *who looks her in the eyes,
silent.*)

Here?

ANNIE: Spell it.

(KATE *spells a word—no—shaking her head;* ANNIE
*spells two words—why, not—back, with an impa-
tient question in her eyes; and* KATE *moves her head
in pain to answer it.*)

KATE: Because I can't—

ANNIE: Spell it! If she ever learns, you'll have a lot to
tell each other, start now.

(KATE *painstakingly spells in air. In the midst of
this the rear door opens, and* KELLER *enters with
the setter* BELLE *in tow.*)

KELLER: Miss Sullivan? On my way to the office, I
brought Helen a playmate—

ANNIE: Outside please, Captain Keller.

KELLER: My dear child, the two weeks are up today, surely you don't object to—

ANNIE [RISING]: They're not up till six o'clock.

KELLER [INDULGENT]: Oh, now. What difference can a fraction of one day—

ANNIE: An agreement is an agreement. Now you've been very good, I'm sure you can keep it up for a few more hours.

(*She escorts* KELLER *by the arm over the threshold; he obeys, leaving* BELLE.)

KELLER: Miss Sullivan, you are a tyrant.

ANNIE: Likewise, I'm sure. You can stand there, and close the door if she comes.

KATE: I don't think you know how eager we are to have her back in our arms—

ANNIE: I do know, it's my main worry.

KELLER: It's like expecting a new child in the house. Well, she *is*, so—composed, so—

(*Gently*)

Attractive. You've done wonders for her, Miss Sullivan.

ANNIE [NOT A QUESTION]: Have I.

KELLER: If there's anything you want from us in repayment tell us, it will be a privilege to—

ANNIE: I just told Mrs. Keller. I want more time.

KATE: Miss Annie—

ANNIE: Another week.

(HELEN *lifts her head, and begins to sniff.*)

KELLER: We miss the child. *I* miss her, I'm glad to say, that's a different debt I owe you—

ANNIE: Pay it to Helen. Give *her* another week.

KATE [GENTLY]: Doesn't she miss us?

KELLER: Of course she does. What a wrench this unexplainable—exile must be to her, can you say it's not?

ANNIE: No. But I—

(HELEN *is off the stool, to grope about the room; when she encounters* BELLE, *she throws her arms around the dog's neck in delight.*)

KATE: Doesn't she need affection too, Miss Annie?

ANNIE [WAVERING]: She—never shows me she needs it, she won't have any—caressing or—

KATE: But you're not her mother.

KELLER: And what would another week accomplish? We are more than satisfied, you've done more than we ever thought possible, taught her constructive—

ANNIE: I can't promise anything. All I can—

KELLER [NO BREAK]: —things to do, to behave like— even look like—a human child, so manageable, contented, cleaner, more—

ANNIE [WITHERING]: Cleaner.

KELLER: Well. We say cleanliness is next to godliness, Miss—

ANNIE: Cleanliness is next to nothing, she has to learn that everything has its name! That words can be her *eyes*, to everything in the world outside her, and inside too, what is she without words? With them she can think, have ideas, be reached, there's

not a thought or fact in the world that can't be
hers. You publish a newspaper, Captain Keller, do
I have to tell you what words are? And she has
them already—

KELLER: Miss Sullivan.

ANNIE: —eighteen nouns and three verbs, they're in her
fingers now, I need only time to push *one* of them
into her mind! One, and everything under the sun
will follow. Don't you see what she's learned here
is only clearing the way for that? I can't risk her
unlearning it, give me more time alone with her,
another week to—

KELLER: Look.

(*He points, and* ANNIE *turns.* HELEN *is playing with*
BELLE's *claws; she makes letters with her fingers,
shows them to* BELLE, *waits with her palm, then
manipulates the dog's claws.*)

What is she spelling?

(*A silence.*)

KATE: Water?

(ANNIE *nods.*)

KELLER: Teaching a dog to spell.

(*A pause*)

The dog doesn't know what she means, any more
than she knows what you mean, Miss Sullivan. I

think you ask too much, of her and yourself. God
may not have meant Helen to have the—eyes you
speak of.

ANNIE [TONELESS]: I mean her to.

KELLER [CURIOUSLY]: What is it to you?

(ANNIE's *head comes slowly up.*)

You make us see how we indulge her for our sake.
Is the opposite true, for you?

ANNIE [THEN]: Half a week?

KELLER: An agreement *is* an agreement.

ANNIE: Mrs. Keller?

KATE [SIMPLY]: I want her back.

(A *wait;* ANNIE *then lets her hands drop in surrender, and nods.*)

KELLER: I'll send Viney over to help you pack.

ANNIE: Not until six o'clock. I have her till six o'clock.

KELLER [CONSENTING]: Six o'clock. Come, Katie.

(KATE *leaving the window joins him around back,
while* KELLER *closes the door; they are shut out.*

*Only the garden house is daylit now, and the light
on it is narrowing down.* ANNIE *stands watching*
HELEN *work* BELLE's *claws. Then she settles beside
them on her knees, and stops* HELEN's *hand.*)

ANNIE [GENTLY]: No.

(*She shakes her head, with* HELEN's *hand to her
face, then spells.*)

Dog. D, o, g. Dog.

(*She touches* HELEN's *hand to* BELLE. HELEN *dutifully pats the dog's head, and resumes spelling to its paw.*)

Not water.

(ANNIE *rolls to her feet, brings a tumbler of water back from the tray, and kneels with it, to seize* HELEN's *hand and spell.*)

Here. Water. W*ater*.

(*She thrusts* HELEN's *hand into the tumbler.* HELEN *lifts her hand out dripping, wipes it daintily on* BELLE's *hide, and taking the tumbler from* ANNIE, *endeavors to thrust* BELLE's *paw into it.* ANNIE *sits watching, wearily.*)

I don't know how to tell you. Not a soul in the world knows how to tell you. Helen, Helen.

(*She bends in compassion to touch her lips to* HELEN's *temple, and instantly* HELEN *pauses, her hands off the dog, her head slightly averted. The lights are still narrowing, and* BELLE *slinks off. After a moment* ANNIE *sits back.*)

Yes, what's it to me? They're satisfied. Give them back their child and dog, both housebroken, everyone's satisfied. But me, and you.

(HELEN's *hand comes out into the light, groping.*)

Reach. *Reach!*

(ANNIE *extending her own hand grips* HELEN's; *the
two hands are clasped, tense in the light, the rest
of the room changing in shadow.*)

I wanted to teach you—oh, everything the earth is
full of, Helen, everything on it that's ours for a
wink and it's gone, and what we are on it, the—
light we bring to it and leave behind in—words,
why, you can see five thousand years back in a
light of words, everything we feel, think, know—
and share, in words, so not a soul is in darkness, or
done with, even in the grave. And I know, I *know*,
one word and I can—put the world in your hand
—and whatever it is to me, I won't take less! How,
how, how do I tell you that *this*—

(*She spells.*)

—means a *word*, and the word means this *thing*,
wool?

(*She thrusts the wool at* HELEN's *hand;* HELEN *sits,
puzzled.* ANNIE *puts the crocheting aside.*)

Or this—s, t, o, o, l—means this *thing*, stool?

(*She claps* HELEN's *palm to the stool.* HELEN *waits,
uncomprehending.* ANNIE *snatches up her napkin,
spells:*)

Napkin!

(She forces it on HELEN'S *hand, waits, discards it, lifts a fold of the child's dress, spells:)*

Dress!

(She lets it drop, spells:)

F, a, c, e, face!

(She draws HELEN'S *hand to her cheek, and pressing it there, staring into the child's responseless eyes, hears the distant belfry begin to toll, slowly: one, two, three, four, five, six.*

On the third stroke the lights stealing in around the garden house show us figures waiting: VINEY, the other servant, MARTHA, PERCY at the drapes, and JAMES on the dim porch. ANNIE and HELEN remain, frozen. The chimes die away. Silently PERCY moves the drape-rod back out of sight; VINEY steps into the room—not using the door—and unmakes the bed; the other servant brings the wheelbarrow over, leaves it handy, rolls the bed off; VINEY puts the bed linens on top of a waiting boxful of HELEN'S toys, and loads the box on the wheelbarrow; MARTHA and PERCY take out the chairs, with the trayful, then the table; and JAMES, coming down and into the room, lifts ANNIE'S suitcase from its corner. VINEY and the other servant load the remaining odds and ends on the wheelbarrow, and the servant wheels it off. VINEY and the children departing leave only JAMES in the room with ANNIE and HELEN. JAMES studies the two of them, with-

*out mockery, and then, quietly going to the door
and opening it, bears the suitcase out, and housewards. He leaves the door open.*

*Kate steps into the doorway, and stands. Annie
lifting her gaze from Helen sees her; she takes
Helen's hand from her cheek, and returns it to the
child's own, stroking it there twice, in her mother-
sign, before spelling slowly into it:)*

M, o, t, h, e, r. Mother.

*(Helen with her hand free strokes her cheek, sud-
denly forlorn. Annie takes her hand again.)*

M, o, t, h—

*(But Kate is trembling with such impatience that
her voice breaks from her, harsh.)*

KATE: Let her come!

*(Annie lifts Helen to her feet, with a turn, and
gives her a little push. Now Helen begins groping,
sensing something, trembling herself; and Kate
falling one step in onto her knees clasps her, kiss-
ing her. Helen clutches her, tight as she can. Kate
is inarticulate, choked, repeating Helen's name
again and again. She wheels with her in her arms,
to stumble away out the doorway; Annie stands unmoving, while Kate in a blind walk carries Helen
like a baby behind the main house, out of view.*

ANNIE *is now alone on the stage. She turns, gazing around at the stripped room, bidding it silently farewell, impassively, like a defeated general on the deserted battlefield. All that remains is a stand with a basin of water; and here* ANNIE *takes up an eyecup, bathes each of her eyes, empties the eyecup, drops it in her purse, and tiredly locates her smoked glasses on the floor. The lights alter subtly; in the act of putting on her glasses* ANNIE *hears something that stops her, with head lifted. We hear it too, the voices out of the past, including her own now, in a whisper:*)

BOY'S VOICE: You said we'd be together, forever— You promised, forever and—*Annie!*

ANAGNOS' VOICE: But that battle is dead and done with, why not let it stay buried?

ANNIE'S VOICE [WHISPERING]: I think God must owe me a resurrection.

ANAGNOS' VOICE: What?

(*A pause; and* ANNIE *answers it herself, heavily.*)

ANNIE: And I owe God one.

BOY'S VOICE: Forever and ever—

(ANNIE *shakes her head.*)

—forever, and ever, and—

(ANNIE *covers her ears.*)

—forever, and ever, and ever—

(*It pursues* ANNIE; *she flees to snatch up her purse, wheels to the doorway, and* KELLER *is standing in it. The lights have lost their special color.*)

KELLER: Miss—Annie.

(*He has an envelope in his fingers.*)

I've been waiting to give you this.
ANNIE [AFTER A BREATH]: What?
KELLER: Your first month's salary.

(*He puts it in her hand.*)

With many more to come, I trust. It doesn't express what we feel, it doesn't pay our debt. For what you've done.
ANNIE: What have I done?
KELLER: Taken a wild thing, and given us back a child.
ANNIE [PRESENTLY]: I taught her one thing, no. Don't do this, don't do that—
KELLER: It's more than all of us could, in all the years we—
ANNIE: I wanted to teach her what language is. I wanted to teach her yes.
KELLER: You will have time.
ANNIE: I don't know how. I know without it to do nothing but obey is—no gift, obedience without understanding is a—blindness, too. Is that all I've wished on her?
KELLER [GENTLY]: No, no—
ANNIE: Maybe. I don't know what else to do. Simply go on, keep doing what I've done, and have—faith

that inside she's— That inside it's waiting. Like water, underground. All I can do is keep on.

KELLER: It's enough. For us.

ANNIE: You can help, Captain Keller.

KELLER: How?

ANNIE: Even learning no has been at a cost. Of much trouble and pain. Don't undo it.

KELLER: Why should we wish to—

ANNIE [ABRUPTLY]: The world isn't an easy place for anyone, I don't want her just to obey but to let her have her way in everything is a lie, to *her*, I can't—

(Her eyes fill, it takes her by surprise, and she laughs through it.)

And I don't even love her, she's not my child! Well. You've got to stand between that lie and her.

KELLER: We'll try.

ANNIE: Because *I* will. As long as you let me stay, that's one promise I'll keep.

KELLER: Agreed. We've learned something too, I hope.

(A pause)

Won't you come now, to supper?

ANNIE: Yes.

(She wags the envelope, ruefully.)

Why doesn't God pay His debts each month?

KELLER: I beg your pardon?

ANNIE: Nothing. I used to wonder how I could—

(*The lights are fading on them, simultaneously rising on the family room of the main house, where* VINEY *is polishing glassware at the table set for dinner.*)

—earn a living.

KELLER: Oh, you do.

ANNIE: I really do. Now the question is, can I survive it!

(KELLER *smiles, offers his arm.*)

KELLER: May I?

(ANNIE *takes it, and the lights lose them as he escorts her out.*

Now in the family room the rear door opens, and HELEN *steps in. She stands a moment, then sniffs in one deep grateful breath, and her hands go out vigorously to familiar things, over the door panels, and to the chairs around the table, and over the silverware on the table, until she meets* VINEY; *she pats her flank approvingly.*)

VINEY: Oh, we glad to have you back too, prob'ly.

(HELEN *hurries groping to the front door, opens and closes it, removes its key, opens and closes it again to be sure it is unlocked, gropes back to the*

*rear door and repeats the procedure, removing its
key and hugging herself gleefully.*

AUNT EV *is next in by the rear door, with a relish
tray; she bends to kiss* HELEN's *cheek.* HELEN *finds*
KATE *behind her, and thrusts the keys at her.*)

KATE: What? Oh.

(*To* EV)

Keys.

(*She pockets them, lets* HELEN *feel them.*)

Yes, *I'll* keep the keys. I think we've had enough of
locked doors, too.

(JAMES, *having earlier put* ANNIE's *suitcase inside
her door upstairs and taken himself out of view
around the corner, now reappears and comes down
the stairs as* ANNIE *and* KELLER *mount the porch
steps. Following them into the family room, he
pats* ANNIE's *hair in passing, rather to her surprise.*)

JAMES: Evening, general.

(*He takes his own chair opposite.*

VINEY *bears the empty water pitcher out to the
porch. The remaining suggestion of garden house
is gone now, and the water pump is unobstructed;*
VINEY *pumps water into the pitcher.*

KATE *surveying the table breaks the silence.*)

KATE: Will you say the grace, Jimmie?

(*They bow their heads, except for* HELEN, *who palms her empty plate and then reaches to be sure her mother is there.* JAMES *considers a moment, glances across at* ANNIE, *lowers his head again, and obliges.*)

JAMES [LIGHTLY]: And Jacob was left alone, and wrestled with an angel until the breaking of the day; and the hollow of Jacob's thigh was out of joint, as he wrestled with him; and the angel said, Let me go, for the day breaketh. And Jacob said, I will not let thee go, except thou bless me. Amen.

(ANNIE *has lifted her eyes suspiciously at* JAMES, *who winks expressionlessly and inclines his head to* HELEN.)

Oh, you angel.

(*The others lift their faces;* VINEY *returns with the pitcher, setting it down near* KATE, *then goes out the rear door; and* ANNIE *puts a napkin around* HELEN.)

AUNT EV: That's a very strange grace, James.
KELLER: Will you start the muffins, Ev?
JAMES: It's from the Good Book, isn't it?
AUNT EV [PASSING A PLATE]: Well, of course it is. Didn't you know?
JAMES: Yes. I knew.

KELLER [SERVING]: Ham, Miss Annie?

ANNIE: Please.

AUNT EV: Then why ask?

JAMES: I meant it *is* from the Good Book, and therefore a fitting grace.

AUNT EV: Well. I don't know about *that*.

KATE [WITH THE PITCHER]: Miss Annie?

ANNIE: Thank you.

AUNT EV: There's an awful *lot* of things in the Good
Book that I wouldn't care to hear just before
eating.

(*When* ANNIE *reaches for the pitcher,* HELEN *removes her napkin and drops it to the floor.* ANNIE
is filling HELEN'S *glass when she notices it; she considers* HELEN'S *bland expression a moment, then
bends, retrieves it, and tucks it around* HELEN'S
neck again.)

JAMES: Well, fitting in the sense that Jacob's thigh was
out of joint, and so is this piggie's.

AUNT EV: I declare, James—

KATE: Pickles, Aunt Ev?

AUNT EV: Oh, I should say so, you know my opinion of
your pickles—

KATE: This is the end of them, I'm afraid. I didn't put
up nearly enough last summer, this year I intend
to—

(*She interrupts herself, seeing* HELEN *deliberately
lift off her napkin and drop it again to the floor.
She bends to retrieve it, but* ANNIE *stops her arm.*)

KELLER [NOT NOTICING]: Reverend looked in at the office today to complain his hens have stopped laying. Poor fellow, *he* was out of joint, all he could—

(*He stops too, to frown down the table at* KATE, HELEN, *and* ANNIE *in turn, all suspended in mid-motion.*)

JAMES [NOT NOTICING]: I've always suspected those hens.
AUNT EV: Of what?
JAMES: I think they're Papists. Has he tried—

(*He stops, too, following* KELLER'S *eyes.* ANNIE *now stoops to pick the napkin up.*)

AUNT EV: James, now you're pulling my—lower extremity, the first thing you know we'll be—

(*She stops, too, hearing herself in the silence.* ANNIE, *with everyone now watching, for the third time puts the napkin on* HELEN. HELEN *yanks it off, and throws it down.* ANNIE *rises, lifts* HELEN'S *plate, and bears it away.* HELEN, *feeling it gone, slides down and commences to kick up under the table; the dishes jump.* ANNIE *contemplates this for a moment, then coming back takes* HELEN'S *wrists firmly and swings her off the chair.* HELEN *struggling gets one hand free, and catches at her mother's skirt; when* KATE *takes her by the shoulders,* HELEN *hangs quiet.*)

KATE: Miss Annie.
ANNIE: No.

KATE [A PAUSE]: It's a very special day.
ANNIE [GRIMLY]: It will be, when I give in to that.

(*She tries to disengage* HELEN's *hand;* KATE *lays hers on* ANNIE's.)

KATE: Please. I've hardly had a chance to welcome her home—
ANNIE: Captain Keller.
KELLER [EMBARRASSED]: Oh. Katie, we—had a little talk, Miss Annie feels that if we indulge Helen in these—
AUNT EV: But what's the child done?
ANNIE: She's learned not to throw things on the floor and kick. It took us the best part of two weeks and—
AUNT EV: But only a napkin, it's not as if it were breakable!
ANNIE: And everything she's learned *is?* Mrs. Keller, I don't think we should—play tug-of-war for her, either give her to me or you keep her from kicking.
KATE: What do you wish to do?
ANNIE: Let me take her from the table.
AUNT EV: Oh, let her stay, my goodness, she's only a child, she doesn't have to wear a napkin if she doesn't want to her first evening—
ANNIE [LEVEL]: And ask outsiders not to interfere.
AUNT EV [ASTONISHED]: Out—outsi— I'm the child's *aunt!*
KATE [DISTRESSED]: Will once hurt so much, Miss Annie? I've—made all Helen's favorite foods, tonight.

(A *pause*)

KELLER [GENTLY]: It's a homecoming party, Miss Annie.

(ANNIE *after a moment releases* HELEN. *But she cannot accept it, at her own chair she shakes her head and turns back, intent on* KATE.)

ANNIE: She's testing you. You realize?
JAMES [TO ANNIE]: She's testing you.
KELLER: Jimmie, be quiet.

(JAMES *sits, tense.*)

Now she's home, naturally she—
ANNIE: And wants to see what will happen. At your hands. I said it was my main worry, is this what you promised me not half an hour ago?
KELLER [REASONABLY]: But she's *not* kicking, now—
ANNIE: And not learning not to. Mrs. Keller, teaching her is bound to be painful, to everyone. I know it hurts to watch, but she'll live up to just what you demand of her, and no more.
JAMES [PALELY]: She's testing *you.*
KELLER [TESTILY]: Jimmie.
JAMES: I have an opinion, I think I should—
KELLER: No one's interested in hearing your opinion.
ANNIE: *I'm* interested, of course she's testing me. Let me keep her to what she's learned and she'll go on learning from me. Take her out of my hands and it all comes apart.

(KATE *closes her eyes, digesting it;* ANNIE *sits again, with a brief comment for her.*)

Be bountiful, it's at her expense.

(*She turns to* JAMES, *flatly.*)

Please pass me more of—her favorite foods.

(*Then* KATE *lifts* HELEN's *hand, and turning her toward* ANNIE, *surrenders her;* HELEN *makes for her own chair.*)

KATE [LOW]: Take her, Miss Annie.
ANNIE [THEN]: Thank you.

(*But the moment* ANNIE *rising reaches for her hand,* HELEN *begins to fight and kick, clutching to the tablecloth, and uttering laments.* ANNIE *again tries to loosen her hand, and* KELLER *rises.*)

KELLER [TOLERANT]: I'm afraid you're the difficulty, Miss Annie. Now I'll keep her to what she's learned, you're quite right there—

(*He takes* HELEN's *hands from* ANNIE, *pats them;* HELEN *quiets down.*)

—but I don't see that we need send her from the table, after all, she's the guest of honor. Bring her plate back.
ANNIE: If she was a seeing child, none of you would tolerate one—
KELLER: Well, she's not, I think some compromise is called for. Bring her plate, please.

(ANNIE's *jaw sets, but she restores the plate, while* KELLER *fastens the napkin around* HELEN's *neck; she permits it.*)

There. It's not unnatural, most of us take some aversion to our teachers, and occasionally another hand can smooth things out.

(*He puts a fork in* HELEN's *hand;* HELEN *takes it. Genially:*)

Now. Shall we start all over?

(*He goes back around the table, and sits.* ANNIE *stands watching.* HELEN *is motionless, thinking things through, until with a wicked glee she deliberately flings the fork on the floor. After another moment she plunges her hand into her food, and crams a fistful into her mouth.*)

JAMES [WEARILY]: I think we've started all over—

(KELLER *shoots a glare at him, as* HELEN *plunges her other hand into* ANNIE's *plate.* ANNIE *at once moves in, to grasp her wrist, and* HELEN *flinging out a hand encounters the pitcher; she swings with it at* ANNIE; ANNIE *falling back blocks it with an elbow, but the water flies over her dress.* ANNIE *gets her breath, then snatches the pitcher away in one hand, hoists* HELEN *up bodily under the other arm, and starts to carry her out, kicking.* KELLER *stands.*)

ANNIE [SAVAGELY POLITE]: Don't get up!
KELLER: Where are you going?

ANNIE: Don't smooth anything else out for me, don't interfere in any way! I treat her like a seeing child because I *ask* her to see, I *expect* her to see, don't undo what I do!

KELLER: Where are you taking her?

ANNIE: To make her fill this pitcher again!

(*She thrusts out with* HELEN *under her arm, but* HELEN *escapes up the stairs and* ANNIE *runs after her.* KELLER *stands rigid.* AUNT EV *is astounded.*)

AUNT EV: You let her speak to you like that, Arthur? A creature who *works* for you?

KELLER [ANGRILY]: No, I don't.

(*He is starting after* ANNIE *when* JAMES, *on his feet with shaky resolve, interposes his chair between them in* KELLER's *path.*)

JAMES: Let her go.

KELLER: What!

JAMES [A SWALLOW]: I said—let her go. She's right.

(KELLER *glares at the chair and him.* JAMES *takes a deep breath, then headlong:*)

She's right, Kate's right, I'm right, and you're wrong. If you drive her away from here it will be over my dead—chair, has it never occurred to you that on one occasion you might be consummately wrong?

(KELLER's *stare is unbelieving, even a little fascinated.* KATE *rises in trepidation, to mediate.*)

KATE: Captain.

(KELLER *stops her with his raised hand; his eyes stay on* JAMES' *pale face, for a long hold. When he finally finds his voice, it is gruff.*)

KELLER: Sit down, everyone.

(*He sits.* KATE *sits.* JAMES *holds onto his chair.* KELLER *speaks mildly.*)

Please sit down, Jimmie.

(JAMES *sits, and a moveless silence prevails;* KELLER's *eyes do not leave him.*

ANNIE *has pulled* HELEN *downstairs again by one hand, the pitcher in her other hand, down the porch steps, and across the yard to the pump. She puts* HELEN's *hand on the pump handle, grimly.*)

ANNIE: All right. Pump.

(HELEN *touches her cheek, waits uncertainly.*)

No, she's not here. Pump!

(*She forces* HELEN's *hand to work the handle, then lets go. And* HELEN *obeys. She pumps till the water comes, then* ANNIE *puts the pitcher in her other hand and guides it under the spout, and the water tumbling half into and half around the pitcher douses* HELEN's *hand.* ANNIE *takes over the handle to keep water coming, and does automatically what she has done so many times before, spells into* HELEN's *free palm:*)

Water. W, a, t, e, r. Water. It has a—*name*—

(*And now the miracle happens.* HELEN *drops the pitcher on the slab under the spout, it shatters. She stands transfixed.* ANNIE *freezes on the pump handle: there is a change in the sundown light, and with it a change in* HELEN's *face, some light coming into it we have never seen there, some struggle in the depths behind it; and her lips tremble, trying to remember something the muscles around them once knew, till at last it finds its way out, painfully, a baby sound buried under the debris of years of dumbness.*)

HELEN: Wah. Wah.

(*And again, with great effort*)

Wah. Wah.

(HELEN *plunges her hand into the dwindling water, spells into her own palm. Then she gropes frantically,* ANNIE *reaches for her hand, and* HELEN *spells into* ANNIE's *hand.*)

ANNIE [WHISPERING]: Yes.

(HELEN *spells into it again.*)

Yes!

(HELEN *grabs at the handle, pumps for more water,* *plunges her hand into its spurt and grabs* ANNIE's *to spell it again.*)

Yes! Oh, my dear—

(*She falls to her knees to clasp* HELEN's *hand, but* HELEN *pulls it free, stands almost bewildered, then drops to the ground, pats it swiftly, holds up her palm, imperious.* ANNIE *spells into it:*)

Ground.

(HELEN *spells it back.*)

Yes!

(HELEN *whirls to the pump, pats it, holds up her palm, and* ANNIE *spells into it.*)

Pump.

(HELEN *spells it back.*)

Yes! Yes!

(*Now* HELEN *is in such an excitement she is possessed, wild, trembling, cannot be still, turns, runs, falls on the porch step, claps it, reaches out her palm, and* ANNIE *is at it instantly to spell:*)

Step.

(HELEN *has no time to spell back now, she whirls groping, to touch anything, encounters the trellis, shakes it, thrusts out her palm, and* ANNIE *while spelling to her cries wildly at the house.*)

Trellis. Mrs. Keller! Mrs. Keller!

(*Inside,* KATE *starts to her feet.* HELEN *scrambles back onto the porch, groping, and finds the bell string, tugs it; the bell rings, the distant chimes begin tolling the hour, all the bells in town seem to break into speech while* HELEN *reaches out and* ANNIE *spells feverishly into her hand.* KATE *hurries out, with* KELLER *after her;* AUNT EV *is on her feet, to peer out the window; only* JAMES *remains at the table, and with a napkin wipes his damp brow. From up right and left the servants—*VINEY, *the two Negro children, the other servant—run in, and stand watching from a distance as* HELEN, *ringing the bell, with her other hand encounters her mother's skirt; when she throws a hand out,* ANNIE *spells into it:*)

Mother.

(KELLER *now seizes* HELEN'S *hand, she touches him, gestures a hand, and* ANNIE *again spells:*)

Papa— She *knows!*

(KATE *and* KELLER *go to their knees, stammering, clutching* HELEN *to them, and* ANNIE *steps unsteadily back to watch the threesome,* HELEN *spell-*

ing wildly into KATE'S *hand, then into* KELLER'S, KATE *spelling back into* HELEN'S; *they cannot keep their hands off her, and rock her in their clasp.*

Then HELEN *gropes, feels nothing, turns all around, pulls free, and comes with both hands groping, to find* ANNIE. *She encounters* ANNIE'S *thighs,* ANNIE *kneels to her,* HELEN'S *hand pats* ANNIE'S *cheek impatiently, points a finger, and waits; and* ANNIE *spells into it:*)

Teacher.

(HELEN *spells it back, slowly;* ANNIE *nods.*)

Teacher.

(*She holds* HELEN'S *hand to her cheek. Presently* HELEN *withdraws it, not jerkily, only with reserve, and retreats a step. She stands thinking it over, then turns again and stumbles back to her parents. They try to embrace her, but she has something else in mind, it is to get the keys, and she hits* KATE'S *pocket until* KATE *digs them out for her.*

ANNIE *with her own load of emotion has retreated, her back turned, toward the pump, to sit;* KATE *moves to* HELEN, *touches her hand questioningly, and* HELEN *spells a word to her.* KATE *comprehends it, their first act of verbal communication, and she can hardly utter the word aloud, in wonder, gratitude, and deprivation; it is a moment in which she simultaneously finds and loses a child.*)

KATE: Teacher?

(ANNIE *turns; and* KATE, *facing* HELEN *in her direction by the shoulders, holds her back, holds her back, and then relinquishes her.* HELEN *feels her way across the yard, rather shyly, and when her moving hands touch* ANNIE's *skirt she stops. Then she holds out the keys and places them in* ANNIE's *hand. For a moment neither of them moves. Then* HELEN *slides into* ANNIE's *arms, and lifting away her smoked glasses, kisses her on the cheek.* ANNIE *gathers her in.*

KATE *torn both ways turns from this, gestures the servants off, and makes her way into the house, on* KELLER's *arm. The servants go, in separate directions.*

The lights are half down now, except over the pump. ANNIE *and* HELEN *are here, alone in the yard.* ANNIE *has found* HELEN's *hand, almost without knowing it, and she spells slowly into it, her voice unsteady, whispering:*)

ANNIE: I, love, Helen.

(*She clutches the child to her, tight this time, not spelling, whispering into her hair.*)

Forever, and—

(*She stops. The lights over the pump are taking on the color of the past, and it brings* ANNIE's *head*

*up, her eyes opening, in fear; and as slowly as
though drawn she rises, to listen, with her hands
on* HELEN'S *shoulders. She waits, waits, listening
with ears and eyes both, slowly here, slowly there:
and hears only silence. There are no voices. The
color passes on, and when her eyes come back to*
HELEN *she can breathe the end of her phrase without fear:)*

—ever.

(In the family room KATE *has stood over the table,
staring at* HELEN'S *plate, with* KELLER *at her shoulder; now* JAMES *takes a step to move her chair in,
and* KATE *sits, with head erect, and* KELLER *inclines
his head to* JAMES; *so it is* AUNT EV, *hesitant, and
rather humble, who moves to the door.*

Outside HELEN *tugs at* ANNIE'S *hand, and* ANNIE
comes with it. HELEN *pulls her toward the house;
and hand in hand, they cross the yard, and ascend
the porch steps, in the rising lights, to where* AUNT
EV *is holding the door open for them.*

The curtain ends the play.)

WILLIAM GIBSON *WRITES:*

"I was born and educated, within limits, in New York City, not setting foot outside it until my majority; the city runs through much of my work, from first publication, a short story in the mid-thirties, to the play *Two for the Seesaw* more than twenty years later. I have lived for the better part of a decade in the Midwest, with interludes in the Rockies, and these are the locales for the poems collected in *Winter Crook* and the novel *The Cobweb*. Twelve years ago I settled in a Massachusetts town, not far from the birthplace of the heroine of *The Miracle Worker*—to stretch the point somewhat—and my chief sortie out is on record in *The Seesaw Log*, a kind of travelogue of the theatre. I have been married for a short quarter of a century, to a girl who swiftly grew into an eminent psychoanalyst, a contributing factor in my sanity, and in recent years we have taken to raising two boys and our voices."